YOUTH MINISTRY
that lasts a
LIFETIME

by Richard Ross

Youth Ministry That Lasts a Lifetime
By Richard Ross
Copyright © 2017 by Seminary Hill Press

Seminary Hill Press (SHP) is the publishing arm of Southwestern Baptist Theological Seminary, 2001 West Seminary Drive, Fort Worth, Texas 76115.

All rights reserved. No part of this book may be used or reproduced in any manner whatsoever without written permission from SHP except in the case of brief quotations embodied in critical articles and reviews. For more information, visit seminaryhillpress.com/licensing/permissions.

All Scripture quotations, unless otherwise indicated, are from the New American Standard Bible® (NASB), Copyright © 1960, 1962, 1963, 1968, 1971, 1972, 1973, 1975, 1977, 1995 by The Lockman Foundation. Used by permission. (www.Lockman.org)

ISBN-10: 0-9988325-7-X
ISBN-13: 978-0-9988325-7-9

Table of Contents

Preface ... 1

Introduction

Chapter 1
Youth Ministry That Doesn't Last a Lifetime
By Richard Ross ... 7

Chapter 2
Teenagers and King Jesus
By Richard Ross ... 17

Chapter 3
A Biblical Anthropology and Teenagers
By Richard Ross, Malcolm Yarnell, and Clement Woo ... 31

Chapter 4
A Biblical Rationale for Youth Ministry and Youth Pastors
By Richard Ross, Jeremy Gengler, and DongLyul Lee ... 49

Chapter 5
Youth Ministry in Thirds
By Richard Ross ... 61

Part 1–Ministry with Teenagers and Their Families

Chapter 6
Biblical Parenting
By Richard Ross ... 79

CHAPTER 7
Families and the Five Functions of the Church
By Richard Ross and Hyeungyong Bak   95

CHAPTER 8
Programming to Impact Families
By Richard Ross   111

Part 2–Ministry with Teenagers as Part of the Congregation

CHAPTER 9
Biblical Relationships in the Congregation
By Richard Ross   125

CHAPTER 10
Congregations and the Five Functions of the Church
By Richard Ross and Jihun Han   139

CHAPTER 11
Intergenerational Programming
By Richard Ross   157

Part 3–Ministry with Teenagers as a Youth Group

CHAPTER 12
Evangelism, Ministry, and Missions
By Richard Ross and Oluwaseun A. Oladipupo   163

CHAPTER 13
Disciple-Making
By Richard Ross   179

CHAPTER 14
Worship and Prayer
By Richard Ross   203

CHAPTER 15
Community
By Richard Ross   215

CHAPTER 16
Youth Ministry Leaders
By Richard Ross and William David Villarreal   227

CHAPTER 17
Planning and Administration
By Richard Ross and Roy Michael Kelly, II   239

Part 4–Epilogue
CHAPTER 18
The Youth Pastor
By Richard Ross and Clayton Ross   255

Bibliography   271

Preface

By Richard Ross

Youth ministry that doesn't last a lifetime doesn't matter very much. Therefore, the most important question never is, "How effective is our church's youth ministry today?" The question always is, "How effective is our church's youth ministry in reaching and transforming teenagers who will adore Christ for a lifetime, completing their unique missions on the earth for the glory of God?"

Slight improvements to current youth ministry will not lead large percentages of church teenagers to live on mission all their lives. Therefore, this book proposes a radically new model of youth ministry. At the same time, this model does draw from some specific elements of youth ministry that have been effective in the past.

Prior Books

This book retains some elements from the book *Student Ministry and the Supremacy of Christ*. Those elements are biblical and clearly related to lifetime faith. At the same time, those elements have been updated and expanded with additional Scripture and recent, credible research.

This book also retains some elements from the book *The Senior Pastor and the Reformation of Youth Ministry*. Again, the elements retained are valuable as facets in a radical new model of ministry. Also, those elements need attention in a book specifically targeted to youth pastors rather than senior pastors. And again, the elements retained have been expanded with new passages of Scripture and new research.

The Authors

A large section of chapter 3 was written by Malcolm Yarnell, research professor of systematic theology at Southwestern Seminary in Fort Worth, Texas. He developed this content as preparation for the Day-Higginbotham Lectures, presented at Southwestern Seminary, March 2-3, 2017. I am very grateful to the lectureship and to Dr. Yarnell for this masterful content.

My coauthor for much of chapter 18 was my son Clayton. We also coauthored the evangelistic resource *The Gospel Napkin* (Seminary Hill Press). As a youth pastor, I presented Clayton—only four days old—to a teenage New Year's Eve lock-in crowd. From that day forward, he has grown up in a youth ministry environment. I am grateful for the contributions his theological background, clear thinking, and life experiences made to the chapter. Clayton also served as the primary reader for the entire book, making valuable improvements in every chapter.

I also am honored to have coauthored various chapters and sections of the book with some very bright and very transformed Ph.D. students at Southwestern Seminary. Hyeungyong Bak; Jeremy Gengler; Jihun Han; Roy Michael Kelly, II; DongLyul Lee; Oluwaseun A. Oladipupo; William David Villarreal; and Clement Woo will each make a significant impact on youth ministry in the U.S. and worldwide.

David Bryant is a valuable mentor in my life. He is the instrument the Father used to lead me into an awakening to the enthroned majesty of King Jesus. Much of the high Christology that ripples through this book can be traced back to David Bryant. His writing and speaking, now multiplied through tens of thousands of church leaders, represents the most hopeful antidote to the Moral Therapeutic Deism filling the American church.

Youth Pastors

For simplicity, this book uses the name *youth pastor* for the one who coordinates the church's ministry to teenagers and their parents and leaders. That title is synonymous with *youth minister*,

minister of youth, student pastor, associate pastor of student ministry, and several others.

Of the terms available, I chose *youth pastor* on purpose. I like the fact that the term gives that leader similar stature with the other pastors of the church. And, the term implies that the leader increasingly performs more roles that are pastoral and fewer that are activity-driven. Finally, the term communicates this leader's growing church-wide ministry as he connects teenagers with the full congregation and pastors the teenagers' parents and leaders.

The term *youth pastor* certainly includes fully funded and partially funded leaders. But it also includes unpaid leaders who have been called of God and commissioned by the church to coordinate youth ministry. Salary is not necessary to be set apart by God for service. In fact, volunteers in such positions are absolutely vital to the Kingdom. Even in the nation's largest Protestant denomination, half the churches have seven or fewer teenagers. And yet, every one of those teenagers deserves a God-called, church-commissioned, and effective leader.

A Paradigm for the Entire Church

This book proposes the most radical shift in local-church youth ministry since the 1950s. For over sixty years, youth ministry mostly has been limited to activities and programs for teenagers. Youth ministry has mostly kept teenagers in a bubble or silo, separate from the full congregation. And, youth ministry mostly has ignored the biblical role of parents as primary spiritual leaders to their children. That older model often saw youth pastors investing their workweek this way:

- 1 hour—investing in parents and families
- 1 hour—drawing teenagers into the full congregation
- 43 hours—providing programs and events for the youth group

Chapter 5 of this book proposes a radically different model of youth ministry. In order to see many more teenagers walking in faith all their lives and completing their unique missions on earth, the model suggests a workweek like this:

- 15 hours—investing in parents and families
- 15 hours—drawing teenagers into the full congregation
- 15 hours—providing programs and events for the youth group

Here are important questions:

- Could this same view of a workweek be effective for every age-group pastor of the church?
- Since the home is the primary location for spiritual impact, should every age-group pastor give a third of a workweek to building spiritually alive homes?
- Since every believer needs deep relationships and ministry opportunities all across the body of Christ, should every age-group pastor give a third of a workweek to immersing an age group in the full congregation?

Perhaps forward-thinking youth pastors are about to make changes that will set new patterns for the entire church. Perhaps 10-year-olds and 90-year-olds will profit from age-group pastors who embrace ministry in thirds. Perhaps all age groups will more consistently introduce people to Jesus and then disciple them into believers who will, for *a lifetime*, love God, love people, and make disciples for the glory of God.

Are you willing to give up "comfortable" youth ministry for a radically new model that is likely to lead many more teenagers to *lifetime* faith?

Introduction

Chapter 1

Youth Ministry That Doesn't Last a Lifetime
By Richard Ross

Let us run with endurance the race that is set before us, fixing our eyes on Jesus.
—Hebrews 12:1-2

Youth ministry that doesn't last *a lifetime* doesn't matter very much.

Church youth ministry should lead to teenagers who will approach the *end* of their earthly lives able to say with confidence, "I have fought the good fight, I have finished the course, I have kept the faith" (2 Timothy 4:7).

Churches cannot conclude they have an effective youth ministry because:

- The attendance is good or even great.
- There are lots of activities.
- The youth ministry is considered to be the best in town.
- The teenagers are happy.
- The parents are happy.
- Powerful church leaders are happy.

The real criteria for evaluating youth ministry is this question: <u>Are we consistently introducing teenagers to Jesus and then discipling them into believers who will, for *a lifetime*, love God, love people, and make disciples for the glory of God?</u> Senior Recognition

Sunday, which celebrates the graduation of high school seniors, is a good time for the entire congregation to consider:

> To what degree will these teenagers spend the rest of their lives loving God, loving people, and making disciples of all nations for the glory of God?

Of course, the majority of 18-year-olds are not even present for Senior Recognition Sunday. That fact raises two other questions:

1. Where are the seniors, still living in our area, who we ministered to as children or teenagers?
2. Where are the seniors living in our area who never even heard the Gospel?

Everyone who evaluates youth ministry needs to ask a new set of questions.

- The issue really is not: How is our youth group doing today? Instead, the core question is: How will our youth group be doing for a lifetime?
- The issue really is not: How is our attendance today? Instead, the core question is: How will their attendance be for a lifetime?

Those who evaluate youth ministry need to lift their eyes to the future. They need to ask,

- Are we seeing significant percentages of our high school graduates active in church in young adulthood?
- Do we see clear indications that most are living as disciples of Jesus?
- In the power of the Spirit, are they joining Christ in bringing His Kingdom on earth?

- Are significant percentages counting all things as loss for the greatness of King Jesus?

The Current Situation

As long as we keep doing what we've been doing, we'll keep getting what we've been getting. That means about half the teenagers will leave the church after high school, and most never will return. Reporting on results from the Sticky Faith study, Kara Powell notes, "Across cultures, a major turning point for young people's faith seems to be high school graduation. Multiple studies highlight that 40 to 50 percent of youth group seniors—like the young people in your church—drift from God and the faith community after they graduate from high school."[1]

But half of church youth abandoning their faith is not the whole story. An additional 40 percent of youth group members will become lethargic church adults, showing little transformation and making little Kingdom impact. Only 10 percent of the teenagers will become world-changing disciples for a lifetime.[2] Thus, the question is never, "Is our current youth attendance acceptable?" The question is, "Is 10 percent of our youth attendance an acceptable number of lifetime disciples?"

David Kinnaman says it this way:

> Much of the ministry to teenagers in America needs an overhaul—not because churches fail to attract

---

[1] Kara Powell, Jake Mulder, and Brad Griffin, *Growing Young: Six Essential Strategies* (Grand Rapids, MI: Baker Books, 2016), 17.
[2] "Research Shows Parenting Approach Determines Whether Children Become Devoted Christians," April 9, 2007, barna.org; Christian Smith, email to Richard Ross, August 20, 2013. Smith was the architect and lead researcher for the National Study of Youth and Religion. Both the Barna study and the NSYR arrived at the 10 percent figure, though they used slightly different criteria. In general, they found 10 percent of church teenagers can express their core beliefs, can lead someone else to saving faith, and choose to embrace Christ's mission for their lives.

significant numbers of young people, but because so much of those efforts are not creating a sustainable faith beyond high school. There are certainly effective youth ministries across the country, but the levels of disengagement among twentysomethings suggest that youth ministry fails too often at discipleship and faith formation. A new standard for viable youth ministry should be—not the number of attenders, the sophistication of the events, or the "cool" factor of the youth group—but whether teens have the commitment, passion and resources to pursue Christ intentionally and whole-heartedly after they leave the youth ministry nest.[3]

Churches may not have to wait until high school graduation to see teenagers drop out. The exodus begins earlier. According to a major Barna study,

> It is too simplistic to blame college for today's young church dropouts. As evidence, many young Christians dissociate from their church upbringing well before they reach a college environment; in fact, many are emotionally disconnected from church before their 16th birthday. The problem arises from the inadequacy of preparing young Christians for life beyond youth group. ... In other words, the university setting does not usually cause the disconnect; it exposes the shallow-faith problem of many young disciples.[4]

---

[3]David Kinnaman, "Most Twentysomethings Put Christianity on the Shelf Following Spiritually Active Teen Years," September 11, 2006, barna.org.
[4]Barna Group, "Five Myths about Young Adult Church Dropouts," November 16, 2011, www.barna.org.

What Went Wrong?

Youth ministry has many shortcomings, and the reasons for those shortcomings are varied. But related to creating lifetime faith, perhaps the most important factor is the very design of youth ministry itself. That design in most churches today is over sixty years old.

In the years immediately after World War II, parachurch organizations such as Youth for Christ and Young Life experienced tremendous growth.[5] The focus of those groups was on evangelizing teenagers outside the church, especially those segments of teenagers the church was not reaching. A hallmark of most parachurch groups was the youth rally, featuring exciting music, creative skits, and young and dynamic speakers. In larger cities, Youth for Christ built large halls for Saturday night rallies that attracted large crowds and featured speakers such as a very young Billy Graham.

Church youth leaders were impressed with the growth and the excitement of the parachurch groups. Wanting that same kind of response in the church, they began to imitate the parachurch groups. The key seemed to be young leaders who could provide high-energy activities and programs specifically with the teenagers. But here is what the church leaders failed to understand:

> A parachurch model that was effective in evangelizing segments of lost teenagers was not effective in giving Christian teenagers a lifetime faith, lifetime Kingdom impact, and lifetime love for the church.

Some of the most significant deficits with the parachurch model are:

---

[5]Thomas E. Bergler, *The Juvenilization of American Christianity* (Grand Rapids, MI: Eerdmans, 2012).

1. Parents are replaced by young leaders as the primary spiritual leaders of teenagers. Parents are relegated to taxi driving and logistical support.
2. Teenagers do not experience the spiritual impact that comes from growing up in a rich web of relationships with the full congregation.
3. Teenagers do not experience a sense of belonging with the full church and do not feel a calling to be a part of the ministry of the full church.
4. Students do not feel drawn toward the church after they graduate from high school, because they grow up mostly cut off from the full church.
5. Teenagers reared on a diet of rallies, creativity, and excitement come to assume those are the heart of one's Christian experience. Intense discipleship and sacrificial service seem unattractive. Walt Mueller notes: "We cloister [teenagers] together with their peers in a trendy room designed to draw and keep them, which might actually promote the irrelevance of anything in the church that exists outside of that room. This is tragic."[6]

Such glaring deficits make it remarkable that the vast majority of churches have embraced the parachurch model for over sixty years. The time for change is long overdue.

Can changing the design of youth ministry today make lifetime faith more common? Absolutely. For example, teenagers who spend almost all their time in a youth silo at church are more likely to walk away from their faith after high school. Teenagers who balance church life between time with peers and time with the other generations tend to walk in faith for a lifetime. Churches who only value attendance today will opt for keeping the teenagers in a youth bubble at church. Churches who value building

---

[6] Walt Mueller, "Why Youth Ministry Shouldn't Be the Greatest Show on Earth," June 1, 2017, cpyu.org.

lifetime disciples will create a balance between youth-only and intergenerational programming.

This book is designed to explore many such changes that can and should be made to typical youth ministry. Soon we may see far more students leaving youth group with a rock-solid faith that will last a lifetime.

A Faith That *Does* Last a Lifetime

Changing the design of youth ministry can lead to more lifetime faith and Kingdom impact. But such change will be even more effective if leaders have a clear picture of the "end product" of their ministry. In other words, leaders need a clear picture of the young believer they pray eighteen years of ministry will lead to.

After studying four hundred representative churches, Eric Geiger and Jeff Borton reported: "In our observations of student ministries, we discovered that most student ministries have not determined what type of student they seek to build. These ministries simply exist, offering programs and events with no sense of direction and no understanding of how the programs contribute to the overall picture."[7] The youth pastor, church leaders, and congregation cannot move forward in youth ministry without a clear understanding of what lifetime faith looks like.

Fortunately, Scripture provides a detailed picture of followers of Jesus. These biblical descriptions should form the foundation for every element of youth ministry:

- Teenagers who love God with all their heart, soul, mind, and strength (Matthew 22:37).
- Teenagers who love others more than they love themselves (Matthew 22:39).

---

[7]Eric Geiger and Jeff Borton, *Simple Student Ministry* (Nashville, TN: B&H Publishing Group, 2009), 37.

- Teenagers who know their identity is in Christ and their purpose is to know, enjoy, and share the glory of God (1 Corinthians 2:2; Isaiah 43:7).
- Teenagers who grasp more and more of the grandeur and majesty of the Son, enthroned at the right hand of the Father (Colossians 1:15-18; Hebrews 1:13).
- Teenagers who worship with awe intertwined with intimacy (Isaiah 6:5).
- Teenagers who abide in Christ as branches infused by the vine (John 15:5).
- Teenagers who embrace the spiritual disciplines and who pray in running conversations with Jesus throughout the day (1 Thessalonians 5:17).
- Teenagers who invite the Holy Spirit to empower their spiritual gifts in order to actively serve the King (Ephesians 5:18).
- Teenagers who increasingly die to self and invite Christ to live through them (John 12:24; Romans 8:9-10).
- Teenagers who know they exist to reflect Christ's sovereign rule and to join Him in bringing His Kingdom on the earth (Philippians 2:10; Matthew 6:10).
- Teenagers who joyfully serve out of gratitude for the Gospel and Christ's completed work—who love Him because He first loved them (Colossians 2:7; 1 John 4:19).
- Teenagers who feel no need to earn what is already theirs (Ephesians 2:8-9).
- Teenagers who so love Jesus that they introduce others to Him (John 1:45-46).
- Teenagers who increasingly become like Christ, thinking His thoughts, sharing His worldview, and demonstrating His sacrificial compassion (Romans 8:29).
- Teenagers who make disciples who make disciples (Matthew 28:18-20).

- Teenagers who risk everything—comfort, possessions, security, family, social status, and their very lives—to be abandoned to Jesus and to make the Gospel known among all peoples (Philippians 3:8).
- Teenagers who have an allegiance to their King that far transcends their allegiance to the culture (Ephesians 1:21).
- Teenagers who know how to search and interpret the Scriptures to discover more of what it means to be a disciple of Jesus (2 Timothy 2:15).
- Teenagers who can articulate, defend, and live out the faith that is in them for a lifetime (1 Peter 3:15).
- Teenagers who look forward to adoring and reigning with King Jesus forever and ever (Revelation 20:6).

Are you willing to give up "comfortable" youth ministry for a radically new model that is likely to lead many more teenagers to *lifetime* faith?

Chapter 2

Teenagers and King Jesus
By Richard Ross

He is also head of the body, the church;
and He is the beginning, the firstborn from the dead,
so that He Himself will come to have first place in everything.
—Colossians 1:8

Youth ministry has its share of shortcomings, but a limited view of Christ may be the most important of all. Until teenagers see and adore Christ as their monarch rather than as their mascot, little else will change.

The Heart

A leader might say, "When I hear what some of our church teenagers have been doing, it's so frustrating. Why can't they live consistently with their beliefs?"

In reality, those teenagers *are* living consistently with their beliefs—their true beliefs—and not necessarily with their professed beliefs. How people behave reveals what they truly believe.

The late Dallas Willard said, "We frankly need to do much less of this managing of action, and especially with young people. We need to concentrate on changing the minds of those we would reach and serve. What they do will certainly follow, as Jesus well understood and taught."[8]

Be always precedes *do*. Or to say it another way, the heart always comes first. According to Willard, "The will, or heart, is the

---

[8] Dallas Willard, *The Divine Conspiracy: Rediscovering Our Hidden Life in God* (New York: HarperCollins Publishers, 1998), 307.

executive center of the self. ... It, more than anything else, is what we are. ... It is the human spirit, and the only thing in us that God will accept as the basis of our relationship to him."[9]

When we consider teenage discipleship and the behavior that follows, we first must consider the heart. A foundational issue in the heart is deep gratitude that follows repentance and grace. Guilty people do not act better; forgiven people do.

But as important as grace and the Gospel are, they are not a teenager's *ultimate* focus. Michael Reeves notes:

> We naturally gravitate, it seems, toward anything but Jesus—and Christians almost as much as anyone—whether it's "the Christian worldview," "grace," "the Bible" or "the gospel," as if they were things in themselves that could save us. ... Other things, wonderful things, vital concepts, beautiful discoveries so easily edge Jesus aside. ... But the center, the cornerstone, the jewel in the crown of Christianity is not an idea, a system or a thing; it is not even "the gospel" as such. It is Jesus Christ.[10]

Intimacy and Awe

Believers respond to grace by abiding in Christ. If a husband talked with his wife for a while every morning but then never spoke to her the rest of the day, that marriage would be empty and dysfunctional. The same is true of a relationship with Christ. If a teenager's branch is connected to the vine, he will be in a running conversation with Jesus from morning to night. Scripture uses the most intimate moments shared by a married couple to illustrate the depth of relationship God desires with believers.

---

[9]Ibid., 80-81.
[10]Michael Reeves, *Rejoicing in Christ* (Downers Grove, IL: InterVarsity Press, 2015), 10.

Teenagers abide in Christ in intimacy, but they should never lose a sense of awe at His greatness. Willard says, "The key, then, to loving God is to *see Jesus,* to hold him before the mind with as much fullness and clarity as possible. It is to adore him."[11]

Leaders guide teenagers toward loving Jesus with all their hearts—hearts filled with gratitude for grace. Leaders guide them to abide constantly in Him and to adore Him with a double helix of warm intimacy and overwhelming awe.

Imitation of Christ

The transforming heart then shapes the individual. Michael Frost and Alan Hirsch say, "(It) is God's unambiguous aim to make us to be more like his Son. In fact, this is our eternal destiny: 'to be conformed to the likeness of his Son' (Romans 8:29)."[12]

The imitation of Christ is intertwined with the adoration of Christ. Jesus said, "If you love Me, you will keep My commandments" (John 14:15). And, according to Jesus, this works both ways. In John 15:10, Jesus says, "If you keep My commandments, you will abide in My love." John 14:23 pulls it all together: "Jesus answered and said to him, 'If anyone loves Me, he will keep My word; and My Father will love him, and We will come to him and make Our abode with him.'"

According to Willard:

> The disciple or apprentice of Jesus, as recognized by the New Testament, is one who has firmly decided to learn from him how to lead his or her life, whatever that may be, as Jesus himself would do it. And, as best they know how, they are making plans—taking the necessary steps, progressively arranging and rearranging their affairs—to do this. All of this will, in one

---

[11] Willard, *Divine Conspiracy*, 334.
[12] Michael Frost and Alan Hirsch, *ReJesus* (Peabody, MA: Hendrickson Publishers, 2009), 13.

way or another, happen within the special and unfailing community he has established on earth.[13]

A teenager who has decided to think and act like Jesus has to know objectively what that means. That comes from Scripture. Speaking to the Father, Jesus said, "Sanctify them in the truth; Your word is truth" (John 17:17). Teenagers carefully study Scripture to know exactly what it means to follow Jesus and keep His commandments. They follow and obey because they love and abide. Self dies little by little because of the One they adore.

But even if young believers love Jesus and know much of His truth, they still will find it impossible to live out His life on their own. Jesus knew this and provided an amazing way for young believers to live His way. God has come to live in us—by giving us His Holy Spirit. According to Kyle Idleman, "Jesus says, 'It's better for you if I go'—because while God with you is good, God in you is better.'"[14]

> In reality, the believer does not live for Christ.
> Christ lives His holy life through the believer.

Because Christ is living His life through the teenager, what the teenager does brings Christ's Kingdom more on the earth—which can only serve to bring great glory to God. In so doing, the teenager fulfills the reason for his existence.

Teenagers and God's Son

Unfortunately, all this collapses if a teenage believer has an erroneous view of God's Son. Since Christ is the cornerstone of Christian experience, a flawed Christology has to lead to a flawed life.

---

[13]Willard, *Divine Conspiracy*, 291.
[14]Kyle Idleman, *Not a Fan* (Grand Rapids, MI: Zondervan, 2011), 91.

Many teenagers in the church value their faith because of the advantages it brings to them. They tend to think Jesus exists to make their lives happier and better.

Teenagers invited to give a public testimony often say, "I just love Jesus. He's always there for me." By that they may mean Jesus is getting them through hard times at home or with friends. And of course, Jesus is in touch with every life challenge they face, and He is omnipotent in His ability to intervene in any situation.

But notice the primary focus of the teenage testimony: "He's always there for *me*." Many believing teenagers tend to know Jesus primarily as a friend who brings *them* good things.

Worst case, some teenagers may see Jesus as their little buddy who rides with them in their shirt pocket. He always is there in case they need to pull Him out to "poof" away some difficulty. But the problem is, teenagers may believe He can be returned to their pocket—conveniently out of sight and out of mind until needed again.

Rick Lawrence says, "Many of us want Jesus to give us more of what we want, we want him to do it fast and make it easy for us, and we want guarantees that our fun won't be compromised if we follow him."[15] Lawrence says we may "end up graduating class after class of young Pharisees—teenagers who are pragmatically associated with the benefits of 'religion,' but not desperately in love with Jesus."[16]

Most church teenagers *are* focused on the benefits of religion but are not desperately in love with Jesus. Thus, most eventually will drift away.

The Glory of Christ Today

Elevating one's self over Christ is nothing new. The angels rebelled in heaven because of self. The root of sin in the Garden

---

[15] Rick Lawrence, *Jesus-Centered Youth Ministry* (Loveland, CO: Group Publishing, 2007), 163.
[16] Ibid.

was self. The functional god of much of the American church now has become self.

This inward belief is evidenced by the outward failure to speak of Christ's current, powerful reign from the throne of heaven and His claim over the hearts and lives of His redeemed people. So they have little need to speak of His current, powerful reign at the Father's right hand.

Today, most teenagers still speak of Jesus, but mostly concerning the days He walked on earth. They are more likely to picture Him sitting on a big rock with giggling children in His lap than reigning from the throne of heaven. Bible lessons and church hallway conversations are almost completely devoid of any focus on the transcendent majesty of who the Son is today.

But that is not the testimony of the Bible. Paul declares:

> He is the image of the invisible God, the firstborn of all creation. For by Him all things were created, both in the heavens and on earth, visible and invisible, whether thrones or dominions or rulers or authorities—all things have been created through Him and for Him. He is before all things, and in Him all things hold together. He is also head of the body, the church; and He is the beginning, the firstborn from the dead ... (Colossians 1:15-18).

At the moment of His return, Christ will appear, more majestic and powerful than anyone can possibly imagine. He will split the heavens. All humanity will see Him for who He is (1 Thessalonians 4). Youth leaders need to ask themselves:

- Do our teenagers know that who Christ will be on that day is precisely who He is today?
- Do they know that His sovereign glory on that day is His sovereign glory now?

- When our teenagers prayed this morning, were they seeing Christ on His throne?
- Do we as leaders really know Him today the way He will be when He returns?

In the Old Testament, God spoke through the prophets, and He revealed Himself in many other ways. Beginning two thousand years ago, He has chosen to reveal Himself most clearly in His Son (Hebrews 1:1-2). This is a perfect plan since the Son is the radiance of God's glory and the exact representation of His nature (Hebrews 1:3).

When the Son had made purification of sins, He was enthroned at the right hand of the Majesty on high (Hebrews 1:3). The Father then announced that in this age of the church, God the Son is to have supremacy (Colossians 1:18).

Leaders have spent decades talking to teenagers about the centrality of Christ but almost never about the supremacy of Christ. Centrality is about keeping Christ at the center of who we are, where we are headed, and all we are doing.

Supremacy speaks of so much more. It proclaims Christ's right to keep us at the center of who He is, where He is headed, and how He is blessed. That teaching could lead to teenage believers who would say, "Jesus does not exist to come down here and make my life a little easier. I exist to stand before Him in awe-filled worship and to join Him in bringing His Kingdom on the earth. It's never all about me. It's always all about Him."

The higher Jesus is lifted, the greater the Father He reveals. In the same way that a rising tide lifts all ships, so too does a rising Christology lift theology, discipleship, lordship, missiology, ecclesiology, and family ministry. A low Christology leaves room for low, vague, and uncompelling theology and church life.

At its root, the Christian faith is a relationship. That relationship is initiated by God, who loves individuals so much He sent His Son to redeem them. The triune God draws them into a relationship with Himself for fellowship and adoration, to join Him in

His Kingdom purposes, and for the display of His splendor. He desires the exaltation of His Son for eternity, not for eighteen years.

Christ created everything, He rules the universe, and He is bringing His Kingdom on earth for the glory of triune God. He is the head of every facet of the church. That means:

> Christ is the founder of youth ministry,
> the goal of youth ministry, and the one who
> should shape youth ministry.

"It is Christology (the exploration of the person, teachings and impact of Jesus Christ) that determines missiology (our purpose and function in the world), which in turn determines our ecclesiology (the forms and functions of the church)."[17]

Where Did Things Go Wrong?

Moral Therapeutic Deism

The National Study of Youth and Religion (NSYR) sent shock waves through the youth ministry world.[18] This in-depth and trustworthy research project discovered that the faith of most church teenagers can be described as Moral Therapeutic Deism (MTD). The core tenets of this belief system are:

- God exists.
- He is nice and He wants us to be nice.
- He is not relevant to my daily life—with one exception. Any time I have a need, He quickly shows up and takes care of that need. Then He goes back to being distant and irrelevant.

---

[17] Frost and Hirsch, *ReJesus*, 6.
[18] See full report in Christian Smith with Melinda Lundquist Denton, *Soul Searching: The Religious and Spiritual Lives of American Teenagers* (New York: Oxford University Press, 2005).

A limited view of Christ (and thus of God) has all the conditions necessary for Moral Therapeutic Deism to thrive and remain unchallenged.

Parents and Church Members

The NSYR study made a second discovery that is just as important. For the most part, teenagers do not reject the faith of parents and important adults in their lives. Instead, they almost perfectly mirror that faith. Christian Smith, architect of the NSYR, reports that teenagers "serve as a very accurate barometer of the condition of the culture and institutions of our larger society. Far from being alien creatures from another planet, American teenagers actually well reflect back to us the best and worst of our own adult condition and culture."[19]

If church teenagers are full of Moral Therapeutic Deism, and teenagers tend to mirror the faith of Mom and Dad, then this is a churchwide issue. Most church teenagers have grown up surrounded by Christian adults who also embrace Christ for His benefits, a Christ who is too small.

Kenda Dean, one of the NSYR researchers, says it this way:

> [The study] is significant because it reframes the issues of youth ministry as issues facing the twenty-first century church as a whole. Since the religious and spiritual choices of American teenagers echo, with astonishing clarity, the religious and spiritual choices of the adults who love them, lackadaisical faith is not the young people's issue, but ours.[20]

Dean goes on to say, "The [study] reveals a theological fault line running underneath American churches: an adherence to a do-good, feel-good spirituality that has little to do with the Triune

---

[19] Smith with Denton, *Soul Searching*, 191.
[20] Kenda Dean, *Almost Christian* (New York: Oxford University Press, 2010), 4.

God of Christian tradition and even less to do with loving Jesus Christ enough to follow him into the world."[21] Then she concludes that "Moral Therapeutic Deism is supplanting Christianity as the dominant religion in the United States."[22]

In the U.S., things first began to go wrong in the 1960s. Believers generally shifted their primary focus to becoming more prosperous, comfortable, and happy. They still held to Jesus, but only as their church mascot and an addendum to pursuing the American dream.

Chasing that American dream has become a spiritual nightmare. Youth pastors can demonstrate the truth of this by asking:

- Are the parents in our church more excited about their children growing in the spiritual disciplines or winning trophies?
- Are our parents more excited about church youth camp or an athletic camp that might lead to a varsity starting position?
- Are they working harder toward a full college scholarship or toward seeing their high school graduate take the Gospel overseas?

Dean summarizes this issue by noting, "[T]he religiosity of American teenagers must be read primarily as a reflection of their parents' devotion (or lack thereof) and, by extension, that of their congregation."[23]

The church Christ founded increasingly has stopped speaking of Him by name, much less His power and kingly reign. When disciples are not shaped by clear language about the majesty of Christ, that sets the stage for MTD, a weak Christology, and the perspective, "It really is all about me."

---

[21] Ibid.
[22] Ibid., 14.
[23] Ibid., 3-4.

For good or ill, teenagers closely resemble the spiritual lives of their parents, youth pastor, leaders, and congregation. If most believing teenagers have an inadequate view of Christ, perhaps some of the key adults in their lives also need to be reintroduced to the real Jesus for all He is.

Your Youth Group

In your church, perhaps that awakening will begin with you. Maybe the Spirit will immerse you in books, Scriptures, and prayer about the current majesty of the Son. Then perhaps your new vision of the enthroned Christ will splash over on parents and other youth leaders. Soon after, maybe you will see your teenagers filled with wonder concerning King Jesus. Then maybe, just maybe, a Christ awakening will spill out of the youth room and will begin to flood the entire congregation.

The fulfillment of every hope and dream you have for your church begins when the Spirit awakens believers to the majesty of the Son for the glory of the Father. You can begin to proclaim to teenagers:

- Your King is not distant. The Holy Spirit is present and living in your heart just as He is seated on the throne of heaven.
- Jesus Christ is not irrelevant. He is at this moment reigning over every element of the cosmos. That includes all that is happening in and around you.
- He is not the divine butler who only lives to make you happy. He is the majestic King who exists for His glory and for the coming of His Kingdom on the earth. He does not primarily exist for you. You exist for Him.

What might happen if teenagers begin to grasp all this? Rather than seeing Jesus as a little buddy tucked down in their pocket, what if they begin to embrace His transcendence and His Kingdom purposes? What if they discover new awe over the overwhelming glory of the triune God as He reveals Himself through His Son?

What if a true awakening to the Almighty begins in the youth group? Could teenagers and their parents and leaders then spark a similar awakening in the full church? Is such a possibility worthy of prayer-filled support?

The Implications of a Christ Awakening

When teenagers and adults begin to determine who Christ really is today, they fall before Him and shout, "Holy, Holy, Holy!" They are overwhelmed and in awe. As they grasp more and more of His surpassing greatness, then it makes perfect sense to count everything else as loss.

Paul says it this way in Philippians 3:7–8:

> But whatever things were gain to me, those things I have counted as loss for the sake of Christ. More than that, I count all things to be loss in view of the surpassing value of knowing Christ Jesus my Lord, for whom I have suffered the loss of all things, and count them but rubbish so that I may gain Christ.

Possessions

People have a huge need to gather and horde possessions. Teenagers want to spend what they have on themselves. What could motivate them to count all things as loss? Their overwhelming love for and adoration of King Jesus is what moves them to release their death grip on what they own.

For teenagers, the "doctrine" of Jesus is not enough to do this. Having a relationship with a "little buddy" Jesus is not enough. Only worshiping Christ in all His majesty and supremacy is powerful enough to move them to count all loss.

If teenagers are deeply in love with Jesus and their hearts yearn to see His Kingdom come on earth, then releasing some possessions isn't a sacrifice. Instead, it's a delight (2 Corinthians 9:7). Giving is a way of expressing overwhelming love to God.

Those who live for Christ alone may choose to creatively downsize their standard of living for the sake of the Kingdom. Simple living can lead to extravagant gifts that help fund getting the Gospel to every person on earth. Those who deeply want all to know Christ find it a joy to commit finances to this purpose.

Simple living also can lead to extravagant gifts that address human need and suffering in the name of Christ. Actually, there is enough money today to feed every person on earth and to get the Gospel to everyone. But for the moment that money is in the pockets of Christians. Wealth in and of itself is not sinful, but greed and selfishness are.

Fame

Our culture is fascinated with fame. Many teenagers believe they will be famous or well-known by the time they reach adulthood. Teenagers see obscure people become famous overnight through viral online videos, reality TV, or talent shows. They assume it may happen to them.

Parents had the best of intentions. They listened to "experts" who said children have fragile self-concepts and thus need to hear they're special many times a day. So that's just what the parents did. They videoed every moment of their children's lives, created nurseries more elaborate than a Disney set, reverently placed every crayon drawing on the refrigerator, and built little shrines around trophies.

Good parents do give healthy attention to their children. But many recent parents have taken this to the extreme. It's little wonder that many grade-schoolers literally rule their homes and dictate many major decisions. No wonder teenagers believe they are the center of things.

Everyone works for someone's fame. The choice facing your teenagers is: "Do I work for my fame or for the fame of King

Jesus, to make Him more famous in my immediate world and in all the nations?"

One's Physical Life

Your teenagers will not likely be called to lay down their lives for the sake of the Gospel. But it is important they let Christ know they would consider it a high honor to do so. Jesus said, "The hour has come for the Son of Man to be glorified. Truly, truly, I say to you, unless a grain of wheat falls into the earth and dies, it remains alone; but if it dies, it bears much fruit. He who loves his life loses it, and he who hates his life in this world will keep it to life eternal" (John 12:23–25).

Use your imagination. Picture a generation of teenagers who love Christ with all their heart, soul, mind, and strength. Picture teenagers who adore the King above relationships, possessions, comfort, and a long life—who absolutely would lay those things down at Christ's command. Picture teenagers who therefore are not bound to the culture. A generation such as that can—quite literally—change the world.

Writing at age 18, Jaquelle Crowe gives this challenge to her generation:

> Be humble, be wonderstruck, be faithful, and throw yourself into a single-focused pursuit of this King of the universe. Take up your cross, deny yourself daily, and follow him. God is at work in this generation. He's raising up young people to reject the status quo and risk everything to obey him. That's our generation. That's me. That's you. And this is our calling.[24]

---

[24] Jaquelle Crowe, *This Changes Everything: How the Gospel Transforms the Teen Years* (Wheaton, IL: Crossway, 2017), 147-48.

Chapter 3

A Biblical Anthropology and Teenagers

By Richard Ross, Malcolm Yarnell, and Clement Woo

God created man in His own image....
—Genesis 1:27a

Youth pastors must know Jesus. And the Word of God. And people. Other chapters will address the youth pastor's knowledge and understanding of parents, leaders, and members of the congregation. This chapter addresses that group of people youth pastors must know and understand best of all—those approximately 12 to 18.

A Biblical Anthropology
By Malcolm Yarnell

Anthropology refers to the study of human beings. Biblical anthropology refers to the study of the biblical view of human beings.[25] How a youth pastor sees a teenager depends on how he sees the human race. How a teenager sees himself depends on the same thing.

In Western cultures, human beings are redefining humanity at a breakneck pace. We have pictured ourselves as little gods who believe we can redefine our being, purpose, and even gender according to the slightest whim of fancy. Sexual perversity and

---

[25]This section is adapted from the Day-Higginbotham Lectures, prepared and delivered by Malcolm Yarnell at Southwestern Baptist Theological Seminary, March 2-3, 2017.

infant murder are on the march, wrapping themselves falsely in the flags of freedom and dignity.

Does mankind have the ability to define the nature of mankind? Of course, nothing could be further from the truth. John Hammett declares, "The most important fact one can state about any human being is that he or she is created in the image of God (*imago Dei*)."[26]

Genesis 1 and 2 give us a picture of the image of God in mankind *in the past*, in humanity's pristine created state. Ecclesiastes 3 gives us a picture of that image *in the present*, with a heart for God but a body bound to earth, expecting judgment. Scripture also provides the picture of the image *in the future* and addresses its redemption and consummation.

The Image of God in the Past

The Creation of Man. A full understanding of humanity must begin with the creation of mankind in the Garden. The inspired author Moses concluded the creature Adam was not merely "good" or "beautiful" like the others, but "very good."[27] According to Luther, "Moses points out an outstanding difference between these living beings and man when he says that man was created by the special plan and providence of God. This indicates that man is far superior to the rest of the living beings that live a physical life."[28]

In this first song, God sang man into existence, pouring Himself into him, making him "in" (*be*) His "image" or "as" His "likeness."[29] The triune God has poured both His unity and complexity, His simplicity and relationality into this exalted creature. The Creator

---

[26] John S. Hammett, "Human Nature," in *A Theology for the Church*, ed. Daniel Akin (Nashville, TN: Broadman and Holman Academic, 2007), 293.
[27] Moses wrote that Adam was not merely *tob*, "good" or "beautiful," like the others (1:12, 18, 21, 25), but *me'od tob*, "very good" (1:31).
[28] Martin Luther, *Commentary on Genesis, Vol. II - Luther on Sin and the Flood* (Minneapolis, MN: The Luther Press, 2010), 56.
[29] "In" (*be*) His "image" (*tselem*) or "as" (*ke*) His "likeness" (*demuth*).

has sung His image, His likeness, into the human. This is a gift no other creature has been granted.

In His being, God is one yet three. The one God, the Lord, is God the Father, the Son, and the Holy Spirit. In His acts, God's work is indivisible even as certain works are proper to the three persons. We can affirm the following works:

- The Father is Ruler.
- The Son is Word.
- The Holy Spirit is Life-giver.

In work, the Father is the Ruler, the Elector, and the Creator. He sends the Son and the Spirit on their respective missions into the world. The Father's proper work is Rule. The Son's proper work is that of Word, of revealing the rule of God. In work, the Holy Spirit does many things, but premier among them is that He creates life and maintains that life as long as He is related to it. The Spirit also creates new life in fallen humanity through the Word.

First, note that when God makes man in His image, He immediately and twice indicates that humanity must rule the world on His behalf (Genesis 1:26, 28). Man's rule as God's vicegerent on earth reflects the Father.

Second, note that when God makes man in His image, He forms him from the dust of the earth from which Adam derives his name. The "breath" or "spirit" of God (Genesis 1:2) breathed "breath," or "Spirit," into the body of Adam, giving him "life" (2:7).[30] As long as the Spirit maintains that breath in humanity, man lives (6:3). When He withdraws, man dies (7:22). Man's life and relations to Creator and creation reflect the Spirit, the breath of God.

Third, note that when God makes man in His image, He opens communication with man through a word of blessing and a word of command (Genesis 2:16-17). God also brings the animals to man, granting man the power to identify the beasts with words (2:19-20).

---

[30] The *ruach*, "breath" or "spirit," of God (1:2) breathed *neshamah*, "breath" or "Spirit," into the body of Adam, giving him *nephesh*, "life" (2:7).

Man's logic and language reflect the Son, the Word of God. The image of God given to teenagers and all humanity reflects the proper works of the Trinity: the Father in dominion, the Spirit in life and relations, and the Son in logic and language.

Two questions face all human beings, including teenagers:

1. "Who are we?" is the question of communal human persons.
2. "Who am I?" is the question of individual human persons.

Both questions must be answered from a biblical perspective. Scripture offers a different set of answers than human cultures. Too often Christians have allowed cultures to set the agenda rather than Scripture.

The Creation of Woman. The creation of mankind as male and female provides the foundation for identity in community. Female and male receive from the Creator a dual identity by grace.

On the one hand, the "female" is created alongside the "male," receiving the image and likeness of God together with the male (Genesis 1:27, 5:2).[31] The gender of each is a form of identity given distinctly to each. The gifts of maleness and femaleness are not in the power of humanity, but in the gift of God. Contemporary claims that one may change one's gender identity is rooted in an idolatry of self. Those claims are a direct contradiction of the grace of gendered identity.

On the other hand, the woman and the man are together identified by God as "mankind" (*'adam*). While the difference of gender creates distinct identities for male and female, the sharing of human nature creates a common identity. Borrowing from Christology, we might say a boy is fully human and fully male, while a girl is fully human and fully female.

Another indication that woman is a gift is found in Genesis 2:18. Apart from woman, man is in a condition that is "not good" or "not

---

[31] "Female" (*neqeba*); "male" (*zakar*).

beautiful."[32] For the man, God's exalted creature, to be "alone" is to be less than what God intends. Rather, companionship between man and woman is God's created intention.

Woman is not a hurried afterthought of God concerning His original creation's deficiency. Woman is a foreordained forethought of God concerning His creature's wholeness. There is nothing in man that can bring woman to pass. He is the entirely passive recipient of a gracious movement that only the triune Creator can plan, speak, and implement. She is a created gift of God.

Man apart from woman lacks this grace, a grace that itself reflects God, for man and woman together have creative potential alongside the Creator. Through procreation, the creature reflects the Creator. And this particular imaging of God requires both the man and the woman. Procreation requires something from the man and something from the woman.

The specific language of another part of God's divine plan is important: "I will make him a helper suitable for him" (Genesis 2:18). The two Hebrew terms here that God uses to describe His plan for man and woman indicate both order and equality, both dependence and contribution, both identity and relationality.

'Ezer means "one who gives aid" or "helper." The term does not indicate inferiority, but a movement toward the other. *Kenegdo* is a derivative of *neged*, which means "before," "against," or "in the presence." Exegetically, "it suggests that what God creates for Adam will correspond to him. Thus the new creation will be neither a superior nor an inferior, but an equal."[33] The wife so binds herself to a man that she will be about him and will live together with him as one flesh. Marriage is an inseparable relationship.

Woman is given by God to man in order to "help" him fulfill the vocation to which God has committed man. Man is to rule the creation for God. He is to serve and protect God's earth. Humanity is empowered to do this freely through righteous communion with this holy God from the motivation of love. In God's pristine

---

[32] *lo' tob*, "not good" or "not beautiful."
[33] Luther, *Genesis*, 175.

order, man provides the lead to woman, and woman helps man fulfill God's commands. All of this brings glory to God.

Adam exercised authority over woman through naming her. And this exercise was carried out in communion with God in a holy, righteous, and loving manner, authoritatively yet with freedom pouring forth from God through the man into the woman. The first man's first exercise of authority over the first woman, his wife, was not done with tyranny, abuse, or neglect. Those will come later as a result of sin. But for now, before the introduction of sin, human authority is exercised in a divine way.

The Image of God in the Present

Now we turn to the question of individual identity in the present. Ecclesiastes 3 helps provide an answer to the central question of teenagers, "Who am I?"

Ecclesiastes 3:11 says, "He has made everything appropriate in its time. He has also set eternity in their heart, yet so that man will not find out the work which God has done from the beginning even to the end." The word translated "appropriate" also means "beautiful."[34]

The beauty that pours forth from God, the glory of God that permeates heaven and earth—this is what brings order out of chaos. The unbearable weight of God's glory is what ultimately supplants the wickedness of angels and men with the righteousness of God.

"The heart" stands for the individual ego; it is simply the person. God's placement of eternity in human hearts indicates there is a deep-seated desire given to every human being that forces him to move upward in his aspirations.

But the verse also says, "yet so that man will not find out the work which God has done from the beginning even to the end." We cannot see the past well, and we cannot see the distant past at all. Moreover, we cannot see even the immediate future whatsoever,

---

[34] The word translated "appropriate" here is *yapeh*, which also means "beautiful." *Yapeh* has resonance with the Hebrew *tob*, "good" or "beautiful," that appears repeatedly in Genesis 1.

much less the end of all things. Unless God reveals His eternal counsel—what Scripture calls the "mystery" of His will—we cannot know the beginning or the end of the world.

Ecclesiastes 3 is a beautiful passage that helps us see who the human being is, particularly with regard to his individual meaning. The passage is both exhilarating and frustrating. The chapter leads to ten conclusions:

1. Humanity under the sun is subject to the vagaries of time, from the swells of life and waves of dangers, and from the moment of one's birth to one's temporal ending in death (v. 2).
2. The best way to live under the sun is to work at that to which God has appointed us (v. 10) and to enjoy what God has given us (vv. 12-13).
3. God has made everything "beautiful" or "appropriate" in its time (v. 11a). Divine providence is the ultimate reality that makes sense of our earthly realities. To fight against providence is foolish (v. 14), and to help humans flourish is wise.
4. Human beings are creatures bound to time, but God has "set eternity in their heart" (v. 11b). We are here under the sun, but God has placed something in the human heart that pulls a person upward.
5. Yet this desire for God cannot be satisfied through human effort (v. 11c). Our time-bound, earthly context severely limits our ability to discern truth, especially concerning that which is past and that which is to come.
6. The human creature is not only aware of and desirous for eternity; he remains bound to time, to this earthly existence. We came from dust, and we return to dust (v. 20).

7. The human creature may be classified as either "righteous" or "wicked" (v. 17). God will hold each of us accountable.
8. Verse 21 questions the fate of the spirit of the children of Adam. Will the spirit go upward to God when a person dies, or will it go downward to the earth? This verse may refer to heaven and hell.
9. For man to enjoy what he can is good here in this world, for he is unable to crack eternity in his own power. Man's knowledge of that for which he longs is beyond his natural grasp (v. 22. See also Ecclesiastes 8).
10. While Ecclesiastes is in the Bible to remind us that natural revelation reveals something about the Creator God and something about His creature, mankind, more revelation is required in order to know the beginning and the end of humanity (v. 11c).

The Image of God in the Future

As noted earlier, Genesis 1 and 2 give us a picture of the image of God in mankind *in the past*, in humanity's pristine created state. Ecclesiastes 3 gives us a picture of that image *in the present*, with a heart for God but a body bound to earth, expecting judgment. Now we turn to the picture of the image *in the future* and address its redemption and consummation.

Romans 3:28 literally says, "a man is justified by faith." The human being is not complete apart from union with the complete human, Jesus Christ. The human being is a human being on the way, and has been on the way since creation. The human being was created in the image of God, and then he marred that image in the Fall. But God was not done.

The Image of Christ. The perfect image of God is Jesus Christ, the eternal Son of God incarnate. Consider these passages:

- John 14:9, "He who has seen Me has seen the Father."
- John 14:10, "Do you not believe that I am in the Father, and the Father is in Me?"
- Colossians 1:15, "He is the image of the invisible God, the firstborn of all creation."
- Colossians 1:17, "He is before all things, and in Him all things hold together."
- Hebrews 1:3, "And He is the radiance of His glory and the exact representation of His nature, and upholds all things by the word of His power. When He had made purification of sins, He sat down at the right hand of the Majesty on high...."

We discover the meaning of the image of God by looking at Jesus Christ. "Christ alone is so clearly the perfect image of God, and thereby expresses human potentiality. ... Jesus Christ is the model and standard of the visible image of God."[35]

The perfect image of God within His deity is the one person, Jesus Christ. The perfect image of God, fully God and fully man, is the person we know as the Son of God.

Christ's perfection as God was brought through His person to bring perfection to humanity through His incarnation, death, and resurrection. In particular, Hebrews 2 points to the role of His sufferings in that perfection of the human image. If you want to see what the perfect man looks like, gaze upon the hideous humiliation of the man hanging on the cross.

Transformation into the Image of Christ. Paul writes in 2 Corinthians 3:18, "But we all, with unveiled face, beholding as in a mirror the glory of the Lord, are being transformed into the same image from glory to glory, just as from the Lord, the Spirit." The word *metamorphoō*, translated as "transformed," indicates that a change is being worked within the human being. The desire for eternal glory that was graciously placed in the human heart in

---

[35] Anthony C. Thiselton, *Systematic Theology* (Grand Rapids, MI: Eerdmans, 2015), 140.

creation can only begin to become a reality in the human heart through the grace of God worked in redemption.

Ephesians 4:22-24 says, "...in reference to your former manner of life, you lay aside the old self, which is being corrupted in accordance with the lusts of deceit, and that you be renewed in the spirit of your mind, and put on the new self, which in the likeness of God has been created in righteousness and holiness of the truth." Paul presents the idea of transformation of the image through the concept of a movement from the "old self" to the "new self," or the "old man" to the "new man."

This perfecting of the image of the Trinity in a believer is not only something that happens to a person by the will of the Father through the power of the Spirit. The perfecting of the image also is required of the believer in Christ. Consider these commands to teenagers and all believers:

- John 13:15, "For I gave you an example that you also should do as I did to you."
- 1 Corinthians 11:1, "Be imitators of me, just as I also am of Christ."
- Ephesians 5:1, "Therefore be imitators of God, as beloved children."
- Philippians 2:5-7, "Have this attitude in yourselves which was also in Christ Jesus, who ... emptied Himself ...."

Final Perfection of the Image of Christ. The image of God is being perfected among the redeemed, but there is a profound sense in which the redeemed must also be brought to final perfection. In the consummation of all things, the glorification of the created and redeemed image will reach its completion.

We do not know exactly what that will mean, but we do know that it will come from the grace of union with Jesus Christ. In the here and now, after the Fall and after the transformative sufferings of the Perfect Image, we have only partial knowledge of the future of the image.

John writes in 1 John 3:2, "Beloved, now we are children of God, and it has not appeared as yet what we will be. We know that when He appears, we will be like Him, because we will see Him just as He is."

Humanity really is a being on the way. We were born into Adam, and we are being reborn into Christ. We don't know exactly what we will be, and we acknowledge we never will be divine. But we have the joyous assurance we will be like God. The reference in 1 John 3:2 is to Christ. However, John is the trinitarian apostle, and the antecedents are Father and Spirit. We do not fully understand who the Trinity is now, but someday *we will be like Him*.

Teenage believers should say, "I can hardly wait!"

The Image of God and Developmental Theories
By Richard Ross and Clement Woo

How one sees God and the origination of man will profoundly affect one's idea of who man is. And that determines one's idea of who teenagers are. Most theories of "adolescent" development use evolution as their foundation and make an assumption that God does not exist. This leads to a very different view of mankind than the one presented in the preceding section.

G. Stanley Hall's theory of recapitulation was highly embedded in evolution. He utilized evolutionary theory to argue that the development of the individual paralleled the development of the human species.[36]

Similar to Hall, Sigmund Freud was heavily influenced by Darwinism. He recalled in his autobiography that "the theories of Darwin, which were then of topical interest, strongly attracted

---

[36]Laurence Steinberg, *Adolescence*, 8th ed. (New York, NY: McGraw Hill, 2008), 14.

me, for they held out hopes of an extraordinary advance in our understanding of the world."[37] Freud praised "Darwinian biologists for demonstrating man's 'ineradicable animal nature.'"[38]

Freud also had a very negative view of religion, as he believed religion "would thus be the universal obsessional neurosis of humanity; like the obsessional neurosis of children, it arose out of the Oedipus complex, out of the relation to the father."[39] Freud saw science as God.[40] Freud changed "God created man in His own image" into "man created God in his."[41] With the non-existence of God, Freud had a low view of man and tended to view mankind as animals.[42]

James Fowler also used the phrase "our nearest relatives in the animal world" to describe our link to animals, which implies that man is not much different from an animal.[43] Theorists after Freud, such as Erik Erikson and Jean Piaget, used the same evolutionary foundations as Freud for their work. They all fail to see mankind as a special creation of God.

According to Scripture, the purpose of a person is to glorify God. On the other hand, the purpose of life according to the theorists is usually to resolve a crisis and advance from one stage to another by personal effort. For example, Freud, Erikson, and Piaget all point to advancing to the next stage of development as man's ultimate purpose.

---

[37]Frank J. Sulloway, *Freud, Biologist of the Mind: Beyond the Psychoanalytic Legend* (Cambridge, MA: Harvard University Press, 1992), 13.

[38]John G. West, *Darwin Day in America: How Our Politics and Culture Have Been Dehumanized in the Name of Science* (Wilmington, DE: ISI Books, 2007), 55.

[39]Mary K. O'Neil and Salman Akhtar, *On Freud's The Future of An Illusion* (London: Karnac Books, 2009), 49.

[40]Hans Küng, *Freud and the Problem of God*, translated by Edward Quinn (New Haven: Yale University Press, 1990), 3.

[41]Antoinette Goodwin, "Freud and Erikson: their Contributions to the Psychology of God-Image Formation," *Pastoral Psychology*. 47 (1998): 101.

[42]West, *Darwin Day in America*, 55.

[43]James W. Fowler, *Stages of Faith: the Psychology of Human Development and the Quest for Meaning* (San Francisco, CA: Harper & Row, 1981), 4.

Fowler believes that man's purpose is to find the meaning of life and move to the upper stages in the faith development process. However, his theory makes no allowance for the supernatural. For example, Paul will not fit in Fowler's faith development theory because his radical conversion immediately changed him from the persecutor of the Word to the preacher of the Word. Fowler's theory also does not have a content or object of faith. He allows the content to be any religion or any "variety of particular symbolic, thematic and imaginal content."[44]

Kohlberg's theory has a basic assumption that morality is related to age. This is contradicted by many stories in the Bible. For example, his theory does not explain why Joseph has higher morality than any of his older brothers, who sold him to Egypt (see Genesis 37).

Even more troubling is the fact that most developmental theorists have altered the biblical definition of sin. Zock notes that "the traditional focus of theology on sin has been misplaced in psychology. ... Instead of the redemption of sin, the genesis of an autonomous conscious self has become the norm and ultimate goal in life."[45]

Blind squirrels occasionally find a nut. Developmental theorists occasionally make observations that are consistent with the way God created things. But wise youth leaders will turn primarily to Scripture in order to understand teenagers, mankind, and the created order.

The Concept of Adolescence
By Richard Ross

Family ministry pioneer Rob Rienow says:

---

[44] Ibid., 99.
[45] Hetty Zock, *A Psychology of Ultimate Concern: Erik H. Erikson's Contribution to the Psychology of Religion* (New York: Rodopi, 2004), 28.

> A new invention is mangling the lives of our children and grandchildren. This new invention is not a cell phone, video game, or tablet. It is adolescence. In the twentieth century we invented a new category of personhood—this foggy, lengthy, aimless period of transition between childhood and adulthood. As a result, thousands of men and women in their 20s and 30s have the outward appearance of being adults but still think and act more like children.[46]

New Testament professor David A. Black agrees:

> It is my conviction that the social theory of adolescence undermines both the Christian understanding of human nature and the way in which Christians analyze moral thought. It underscores the modern disinclination to treat a person as responsible for his or her actions. When we assert the "fact" that teenagers are to act like children rather than adults, it becomes a self-fulfilling prophecy.[47]

According to Johnny Derouen, the word *adolescence*, Latin for *adolescere* (to grow up), came into being in the 1400s. It was not commonly used to represent an age grouping until the early 1900s, through the impact of G. Stanley Hall's book, *Adolescence*.[48] Hall and others had a view of the teenage years that was sharply different from previous generations. Derouen provides this snapshot of teenagers before Stanley Hall came on the scene:

---

[46]Rob Rienow, "Foreword," in Richard Ross, *Accelerate: Parenting Teenagers Toward Adulthood* (Bloomington, IN: CrossBooks, 2013), vii.
[47]David Black, *The Myth of Adolescence* (Yorba Linda, CA: Davidson Press, 1999), 17.
[48]Richard Ross, *Accelerate*, 10.

> At 17, your great-grandfather likely plowed all day behind a mule and then went home to help with the baby. Your great-grandmother worked just as hard and just as competently. At 16 she washed clothes by hand with soap she had made, cooked from a fire she had built, roasted chickens she raised herself, took care of the children, planted her own garden, and still had time to care for her husband. Both performed well in their roles because adults had invested years preparing them for just that.[49]

For most of human history, children learning and working alongside parents and other adults transitioned to adulthood by their early to late teens. In the Middle Ages, adult apprenticeships began as young as 7. Young people married soon after puberty and set up independent households.

Many developments led the culture to perceive a new stage of life called adolescence. That stage of life was the creation of modern industrialization, child labor laws, school systems, and other factors emerging between 1880 and 1920. New laws and cultural practices began to separate teenagers from adults.

For most contemporary adults, the concept of adolescence implies extended childhood, marking time, hanging out, and dwelling in a Neverland between childhood and adulthood. In that regard, the concept of adolescence is not helpful to the Kingdom. The concept impedes families and churches as they seek to rear young adults who are motivated and prepared *today* to fulfill their unique missions on the earth.

For many teenage believers, their faith now is an underdeveloped, "adolescent" faith. Most set this weak faith aside during adulthood. Thus, most are not fulfilling their unique calling and mission on earth and not bringing glory to God.

---

[49]Ibid., 9.

Professor Alvin Reid notes, "Moses, Paul, John, and others went from childhood to adulthood. Were they ever teenagers? Yes. But they were never adolescents."[50]

David Black adds, "According to the Bible, the teen era is not a 'time-out' between childhood and adulthood. It is not primarily a time of horseplay. ... The Bible treats teens as responsible adults, and so should we."[51]

Chapter 4 will make clear that the ages of approximately 12 to 18 represent a distinct stage. Some of the ministry of the church needs to be laser-focused on the unique needs and challenges of those in this distinct stage. But a biblically sound perspective will approach them as a distinct grouping of young adults rather than a grouping of leftover children.

Do Hard Things

Challenging teenagers to do hard things for the Kingdom would mark a big change in most church youth ministries. Researcher David Kinnaman asks:

> Is it possible that our cultural fixation on safety and protectiveness has also had a profound effect on the church's ability to disciple the next generation of Christians? Are we preparing them for a life of risk, adventure, and service to God—a God who asks that they lay down their lives for his Kingdom? Or are we churning out safe, compliant Christian kids who are either chomping at the bit to get free or huddling in the basement playing [video games] for hours on end, terrified to step out of doors?[52]

---

[50] Alvin Reid, *Raising the Bar* (Grand Rapids, MI: Kregel Publications, 2004), 58.
[51] David Black, *The Myth of Adolescence*, 22.
[52] David Kinnaman, *You Lost Me* (Grand Rapids, MI: Baker Publishing, 2011), 97.

Kinnaman answers his own questions when he says, "Life without some sense of urgency—a life that is safe, incubated, insular, overprotected, consumptive—is not worth living. The next generation is aching for influence, for significance, for lives of meaning and impact."[53]

Alvin Reid adds, "Youth today are inventing computer games, playing in the NBA, winning gold in the Olympics, and dying as martyrs. Churches must increase the level of expectations that we have for them."[54]

Greg Stier fills arenas across the U.S., training teenagers to share their faith. He reports: "As I travel the nation, I encounter teenagers everywhere who are sick and tired of typical church and dying instead for authentic Christianity. Students all over the nation are crying out for something real. They want a driving cause to live for, and if necessary, to die for. They are tired of the traditional. They long for the radical."[55]

Bottom line, teenagers in most churches tend to be seriously under-challenged. That is sad because, right now, many teenagers are primed and ready to do hard things, to take on grand challenges. They fully are capable of joining Paul in saying, "For to me, to live is Christ and to die is gain" (Philippians 1:21).

Teenage believers need to be challenged year-round, but a summer mission trip provides a unique opportunity to stretch young people. The primary goal for every mission trip must be leading people to Christ, getting converts established in a discipleship process, and planting churches. But the secondary goal can be deepening teenagers through an experience that is hard.

The youth pastor and the core youth leaders might discuss:

---

[53]Ibid., 106.
[54]Alvin Reid, *Raising the Bar*, 34.
[55]Greg Stier, *Outbreak: Creating Contagious Youth Ministry through Viral Evangelism* (Chicago, IL: Moody, 2002), 21.

1. Is it possible a secular club at the high school is doing more to confront some wrong in our area than our church youth group?
2. Is it possible a single teenager in the community has mobilized more support for some cause than a church filled with teenagers, parents, and leaders?
3. Is it possible teenagers who visit the youth group are surprised that they hear lots of announcements about entertainment but none about helping people in the name of Christ?
4. Do we believe that, over time, our teenagers might be more motivated to participate because we challenge them than because we entertain them?
5. Do we call teenagers to perform missions, ministry, and evangelism in ways that sometimes carry a reasonable degree of challenge, risk, and adventure?
6. To head off resistance from overprotective parents, do we need to create more opportunities for parents and teenagers to take on challenges together?

As teenagers, brothers Alex and Brett Harris served as visible spokespersons for a generation ready to do hard things. At age 19, they wrote:

> We're not rebelling against institutions or even against people. Our uprising is against a cultural mind-set that twists the purpose and potential of the teen years and threatens to cripple our generation. Our uprising won't be marked by mass riots and violence, but by millions of individual teens quietly choosing to turn the low expectations of our culture upside down.[56]

---

[56] Alex and Brett Harris, *Do Hard Things* (Colorado Springs, CO: Multnomah Books, 2008), 25.

Chapter 4

A Biblical Rationale for Youth Ministry and Youth Pastors

By Richard Ross, Jeremy Gengler, and DongLyul Lee

And He gave some as apostles, and some as prophets, and some as evangelists, and some as pastors and teachers....
—Ephesians 4:11

Is there a biblical rationale for youth ministry *as it is most commonly conducted* in the U.S.? Is there a biblical rationale for the position of youth pastor *as it is most commonly practiced* in the U.S.? The answer to both questions is "no."

Is there an approach to youth ministry that *is* biblical? Is there a role for the youth pastor that *is* biblical? The answer to both questions is a resounding "yes."

Chapter 3 reviewed cultural changes that took place from approximately 1880 to 1920. These changes in such areas as industrialization, urbanization, and mechanization altered perceptions concerning people 12 to 17 and formed the modern concept of the teenage years.[57]

These historical facts lead to a central question. Does the fact that secular culture created a distinct new teenage period of life provide a rationale for the church to provide targeted ministry to this age group? The answer is "no." Cultural shifts and changes do not determine the nature and ministry of the church. Only the Bible determines that nature and ministry.

---

[57] For a full discussion concerning such social changes, see Richard Ross, ed., *Accelerate: Parenting Teenagers Toward Adulthood* (Nashville, TN: LifeWay, 2015).

War, persecution, gender confusion, economic depression, and a multitude of other changes in the culture impact the church and often require a response from the church. But the shifting sands of culture do not determine the nature of the global or local body of Christ. The sole authority related to the nature and design of the church is the Word of God.

Many youth ministries subtly communicate to teenagers that church youth leaders are their primary spiritual leaders. Those ministries give almost no effort to calling out, equipping, or supporting parents as primary spiritual leaders. Also, many youth ministries keep teenagers in a youth group bubble for six or seven years, leading to limited relationships with the congregation or ministering side-by-side with the generations. Senior pastors, youth pastors, and other church leaders maintain those approaches because they seem to have pragmatic value, even though they do not have biblical support.

Chapter 6 presents a biblical case for parents as the primary spiritual leaders of their children. Of course, not all believing teenagers have believing parents. And not all believing parents have teenagers who will accept their leadership. But God's normative design places parents in first position. Therefore, youth ministry that embraces parents in first position and equips and supports parents for that role is, in that regard, biblical.

Chapter 9 presents a biblical case for teenagers viewing the full congregation as their spiritual family, sharing heart connections with many believers of all generations, and consistently performing the functions of the church side by side with all age groups. Therefore, youth ministry that weekly is bonding teenagers with the congregation and mobilizing teenagers to minister with the congregation is, in that regard, biblical.

Youth ministry that consistently supports parents as primary spiritual leaders is biblical. Youth ministry that consistently bonds teenagers with the full church is biblical. The remaining question is this: Is youth ministry that also accomplishes the mission of the church through teenage-specific ministries biblical? When teenage-specific ministries are balanced with a focus on families and the congregation, the answer is a resounding "yes."

Biblical Recognition of Youth as a Life Stage

Old Testament Support

In the Old Testament, God acknowledges the various stages of life and growth. Ezekiel 16:4-6 provides the clearest example. The earliest part of Jerusalem's history, Ezekiel 16:4-6, is depicted as infancy. Metaphors used to describe this period of development are birth (v. 4); severed umbilical cord (v. 4); the post-birth procedures of cleansing, disinfecting, and covering (v. 4); and being covered in blood (v. 6).

The second part of Jerusalem's history, Ezekiel 16:7a, is depicted as childhood. The metaphor used to describe this period is a plant. Yahweh said to Jerusalem, "I made you numerous like plants of the field." As with children, plants require great care, cultivation, and protection.

Ezekiel 16:7b depicts the third part of Jerusalem's history—the pre-age-of-love years. The metaphors used to describe this period of development are growth, increase in height, full adornment, fully formed breasts, and increase in hair length.

Ezekiel 16:8—the adult years—depict the fourth part of Jerusalem's history. The metaphors used to describe this period of development are "time of love," "skirt," and "nakedness" (v. 8). Thus, the chronological stages of human growth and development depicted in Ezekiel 16 are infancy (vv. 4, 6), childhood (v. 7), pre-age-of-love, i.e., teenagers (v. 7b), and age of love (v. 8).

The Hebrew words translated *youth* also indicate the Old Testament sees youth as a distinct life stage. *Na'ar* references an age range between weaning and marriageable young manhood. *Na'uwr*, a derivative, references an early, immature, vigorous, and trainable stage of life.

The majority of Old Testament references to youth signify a younger, more vigorous time of life. But in the midst of this vigor, which is relatively temporary, there is also great caution to be exercised. Key passages include (emphasis added):

- The intention of man's heart is evil from his *youth* (Genesis 8:21).
- A woman could make a vow to the Lord while living in her father's house—while she was in her *youth* (Numbers 30:3, 16).
- The psalmist declared that God had taught him from his *youth* (Psalm 71:17).
- Solomon declared: "Rejoice, young man, during your childhood, and let your heart be pleasant during the days of *young manhood*. And follow the impulses of your heart and the desires of your eyes. Yet know that God will bring you to judgment for all these things. So, remove grief and anger from your heart and put away pain from your body, because childhood and the prime of life are fleeting" (Ecclesiastes 11:9-10).
- Solomon said people should remember their Creator in the days of their *youth* (Ecclesiastes 12:1).
- Spiritual growth that begins during the time of youth has a tendency to have lifelong impact. Psalm 71:5, 17 says, "For You are my hope; O Lord God, You are my confidence from my *youth*. ... O God, You have taught me from my *youth*, and I still declare your wondrous deeds."

New Testament Support

The recognition of youth as a life stage continues into the Greek New Testament. The Greek words associated with youth are *neotes*—a period of time when one is young—and *paida*—a term that refers to pre-pubescent youth including infants, growing children, and 12-year-olds. The New Testament passages carrying these terms include (emphasis added):

- The rich young ruler told Jesus he had kept the Ten Commandments from his *youth* (Mark 10:20; Luke 18:21).
- Eutychus, a *youth*, was taken away alive after falling to his death during one of Paul's sermons (Acts 20:12).
- Paul's manner of life from his *youth* was known by all the Jews (Acts 26:4).
- Paul advised Timothy to let no one despise him because of his *youth* (1 Timothy 4:12).
- Paul advised Timothy to flee *youthful* passions (2 Timothy 2:22).

A few leaders call for the abolition of all teenage-specific ministry and programming through the church. Those leaders tend to believe that a teenager's total church life should be experienced only with his or her family. Several statements by Jesus suggest a different way ministry can be viewed and conducted toward the younger generations. Those statements include:

- "Do not think that I came to bring peace on the earth; I did not come to bring peace, but a sword. For I came to set a man against his father, and a daughter against her mother, and a daughter-in-law against her mother-in-law; and a man's enemies will be the members of his household. He who loves father or mother more than Me is not worthy of Me; and he who loves son or daughter more than Me is not worthy of Me" (Matthew 10:34-37).
- "If anyone comes to Me, and does not hate his own father and mother and wife and children and brothers and sisters, yes, and even his own life, he cannot be My disciple" (Luke 14:26).
- "Then His mother and His brothers arrived, and standing outside they sent word to Him and called Him. A crowd was sitting around Him, and they said to Him,

'Behold, Your mother and Your brothers are outside looking for You.' Answering them, He said, 'Who are my mother and my brothers?' Looking about at those who were sitting around Him, He said, 'Behold My mother and My brothers! For whoever does the will of God, he is My brother and sister and mother'" (Mark 3:31-35).
- "And He said to them, 'Truly I say to you, there is no one who has left house or wife or brothers or parents or children, for the sake of the kingdom of God, who will not receive many times as much at this time and in the age to come, eternal life'" (Luke 18:29-30).

Bible scholar Craig Blomberg writes, "Devotion to family is a cardinal Christian duty but must never become absolute to the extent that devotion to God is compromised."[58] Biblically sound loyalty to God's family even transcends loyalty to one's earthly family. Concerning a young generation, parents and the church family share the privilege and the responsibility for spiritual nurture. Sometimes that church nurture is best done through a specific focus on an age group.

Scripture clearly delineates three pre-adult age-group categories as objects for intentional ministry: infancy, childhood, and pre-age-of-love (teenagers). Exegesis also reveals that biblical ministry within each of these categories requires a joint effort on the part of the home and the church. The dynamic interplay between home and church is slightly different for each category, but effort from both institutions is required in order to accomplish biblical ministry.

Throughout the biblical period, God called teenagers, and by God's hand, they did amazing things. Many examples in Scripture indicate that teenagers are no longer children but can be taught to assume responsibilities and duties as young adults. Biblical writers

---

[58]Craig Blomberg, "Matthew," *The New American Commentary*, Vol. 22 (Nashville, TN: Broadman and Holman Publishers, 1992), 181.

recognized that the youth years were a unique time of life with unique strengths as well as challenges. Ministry that does the same today has a biblical foundation.

Concerning youth ministry today, Cole and Nielson declare:

> It is good and helpful to provide targeted, age-specific ministries to teenagers. [The teenage period] is a challenging and formative stage of life where students are no longer children, but they are not yet adults. It is important for teens to have a safe place in the church where they can experience Christian fellowship, ask hard questions, and open up the Scriptures with their peers and Christian adults who care about them.[59]

Biblical Rationale for the Position of Youth Pastor

Old Testament Support

Youth pastors can find the roots for their vocation in the pages of the Old Testament. During the period of the exile, the Israelites built synagogue schools to teach their children Hebrew so they would be able to read the Torah. The Israelites recognized the teenage years as an important turning point of life. Consequently, teenagers were taught to "control their own desires, accept responsibility for mature religious actions, and assume adult community responsibilities."[60]

Biblical support for the position of youth pastor also can be found in the priests' educational role among the Israelites. Young Levites (the equivalent of youth) were apprenticed by the older priests (the equivalent of youth pastors) from an early age. The company of the prophets led by Elisha in 2 Kings 4:38 demonstrates another

---

[59] Cameron Cole and Jon Nielson, *Gospel-Centered Youth Ministry* (Wheaton, IL: Crossway Publishers, 2016), 100.
[60] Reid, *Raising the Bar*, 186.

type of youth-focused educational group that was present in the Old Testament.

Samuel also could be a model for youth ministry. God called Samuel to follow, obey, and serve Him at an early age. Samuel served God in the temple and was mentored by the priest Eli. The word *nă'ăr* is used for Samuel's age in 1 Samuel 2:18. Josephus assumed that Samuel might have been 12 years old at that time. When Samuel grew old and gray, he declared that it was from his early age that he served God and led the people of Israel (1 Samuel 12:2).

All of these Old Testament groups or institutions for communicating values and instilling faith into the next generation can serve as a model for modern youth ministries and youth pastors. The same is true in the New Testament.

New Testament Support

According to many scholars, most disciples of Jesus were teenagers when Jesus began His public life and then called them for the ministry. In Matthew 17:24-27, a tax collector asked Peter why Jesus did not pay taxes. Jesus "asserted his independence ... but he was willing to pay the tax in order to avoid giving offence."[61] Jesus commanded Peter to take a shekel from the caught fish's mouth and give it to the tax collector as payment for Jesus and Peter. At that time, "all Israelite males over the age of twenty paid this tribute annually for the upkeep of the Jerusalem temple."[62] In light of this historical reality, if the shekel paid for only Peter and Jesus, then the other disciples had to be teenagers, since they were apparently excluded from paying the tax.

In 2 Timothy 2:2, Paul wrote to Timothy, "The things which you have heard from me in the presence of many witnesses, entrust these to faithful men who will be able to teach others also." This passage is a model for youth ministry today. Youth pastors, as

---

[61]D.A. Carson et al., eds., *New Bible Commentary: 21st Century Edition*. 4th ed. (Downers Grove, IL: InterVarsity Press, 1994), 927. Logos.
[62]Blomberg, "Matthew," 269.

mature believers, can teach and equip a group of teenagers with sound doctrine in order to prepare them for Kingdom impact. They join Old and New Testament leaders who called out teenagers "to invest in with the purpose of expanding God's Kingdom through them."[63]

The Offices of the Church. The Bible provides for two specific offices in local churches: elders and deacons. In the New Testament, the word *diakonos* is translated as "servant," "minister," and occasionally "deacon." The deacons in the New Testament cared for the physical needs of church members and supported the ministries of the apostles so that the apostles could focus on their particular responsibilities of prayer and ministry of the Word of God.

In addition to the office of deacon, Scripture provides for the *presbyteros*, or office of elder, pastor, or bishop. The New Testament uses these terms interchangeably.[64] Pastors were designated for a specific ministry in the church. They were charged mainly with the oversight, government, and guidance of the church, and especially the ministry of the Word.

Paul presented the qualifications of pastors in 1 Timothy 3:1-7 and in Titus 1:5-9. These qualifications can be classified under three main categories. The first category is character. Pastors should be "blameless and above reproach, not overbearing, temperate, self-controlled, respectable, hospitable, able to teach, not given to much wine, not violent but gentle, not quarrelsome, well reputed (particularly among outsiders), upright, holy, and disciplined."[65]

The second category is family. Pastors should be the husband of one wife and a good manager of his family (that is, his children should obey him). Although a pastor is not required to be married and have children—as seen in Paul, Barnabas, and Timothy—a

---

[63]Michael Anthony and Michelle Anthony, *A Theology for Family Ministries* (Nashville, TN: B&H Academic, 2011), 233.
[64]Mark Dever, *Nine Marks of a Healthy Church* (Wheaton, IL: Crossway, 2004), 54.
[65]Ibid., 55.

pastor who is married must be faithful to his spouse and lead his children well.

The third category is the ability to teach and defend God's Word. The essence of the pastor's role is found in teaching. In Titus 1:9, Paul clearly provided the core role of pastors as "holding fast the faithful word which is in accordance with the teaching, so that he will be able both to exhort in sound doctrine and to refute those who contradict." Paul also stated in 1 Timothy 3:2 that a pastor should be "able to teach." As seen in these passages, a pastor must have a complete understanding of "the basics of the gospel as well as the great truths of Scripture, especially those that are under assault in one's own day."[66]

Not only should pastors be qualified by their biblical teaching, but they should be qualified by their biblical life. A pastor should be an example in his daily life for others to follow. Pastors must be the model of biblical life including "their own personal relationship with God in Bible reading, prayer, and worship."[67]

Multiple Pastors. Paul followed the normal procedure of the time and established a *group* of pastors in each church as seen in Acts 14:23. In addition, Paul instructed his spiritual son Titus to appoint elders (plural) in local churches (Titus 1:5). The leader of the Jerusalem church, James, also taught his Christian readers to "call for the elders of the church and they are to pray over him, anointing him with oil in the name of the Lord" (James 5:14).

That the Israelite people in the Old Testament and churches in the New Testament were generally led by multiple elders or pastors indicates that a team of elders or pastors were involved in leadership. Among them, some would naturally undertake and lead more in some ministries than others. For example, Paul wrote in Ephesians 4:11-12 that Christ made some to be apostles, some to be evangelists, and some to be pastors and teachers. This passage

---

[66]Ibid., 56.
[67]Wayne A. Grudem, *Making Sense of the Church: One of Seven Parts from Grudem's Systematic Theology* (Grand Rapids, MI: Zondervan, 2011), 94.

indicates that offices in New Testament churches had different roles for the same purpose of building up the body of Christ.

Understood in this context, although the terms "assistant pastor" and "associate pastor" were not used in Scripture, some pastors probably oversaw certain ministries more than others. Today, these areas can involve children's ministry, youth ministry, adult ministry, music ministry, and others. These ministers should be equally qualified according to the biblical requirements for pastors, and they should lead their ministries according to biblical principles. In so doing, they can take care of specific areas in a church—including youth ministry—for the sake of the body of Christ. The contemporary youth pastor is consistent with a New Testament ecclesiology.

Chapter 5

Youth Ministry in Thirds

By Richard Ross

*We are to grow up in all aspects
into Him who is the head, even Christ....*
—Ephesians 4:15b

If most youth pastors were to stop doing about two-thirds of what they were doing, churches might begin producing more lifetime disciples of Jesus. Why? Because if they stop doing some things, then they will have time to do other things that offer even more promise.

The great majority of youth pastors love King Jesus supremely, embrace their calling fully, and do their work tirelessly. But the time has come for their workweeks to change.

Though their numbers are not great, twentysomething disciples do exist. Those walking in faith, loving the church, and making a difference in the world tend to share three characteristics:

1. They were reared by parents who adored Jesus, loved the church, and were on mission to see Christ's Kingdom come on earth.
2. They grew up with a rich web of relationships with the full congregation and were on mission with church members of all ages.
3. They were in a Bible-drenched youth group led by a youth pastor and leaders who carried the aroma of Jesus.

This book presents a strong biblical case for ministering to teenagers through families, in concert with the full body of Christ, and in age-specific programming. The voice of Scripture outweighs any other considerations. But it is interesting to note that the most reliable studies regarding lifetime faith coalesce around these same three arenas. Those Scriptures and studies are presented in each of the chapters of this book.

We now know the three arenas of ministry most likely to lead to lifetime disciples. Therefore, forward-thinking youth pastors might consider the following workweeks:

1. Approximately fifteen hours a week accelerating the spiritual impact of the homes where his teenagers live.
2. Approximately fifteen hours a week immersing every teenager in the full life and ministry of the congregation.
3. Approximately fifteen hours a week leading what we traditionally have considered youth ministry.

For the more visually inclined, consider it this way:

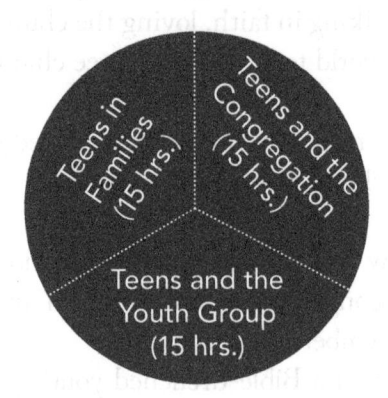

Teens in Families (15 hrs.) | Teens and the Congregation (15 hrs.) | Teens and the Youth Group (15 hrs.)

Of course, ministry is never that neat and tidy time-wise. But these broad hourly divisions point to a significant shift in the youth pastor's role. The fifteen-hour blocks include administrative planning, public leadership, and one-on-one ministry. Each of these three arenas of ministry merits attention.

The Three Arenas of Youth Ministry

Accelerating the Spiritual Impact of Parents

Spiritually lethargic parents suck the power from church youth ministry. Spiritually alive parents intensify that ministry. Spiritually lethargic parents create spiritually lethargic young adults. Spiritually alive parents create young disciples who join King Jesus in changing the world.

The following might be an exaggeration, but some church parents seem to have these "discipleship" goals for their church's youth ministry:

1. Make church so fun that my Precious will come without giving me hassle at home.
2. Motivate sweet Precious to succeed and make a good living.
3. Keep my Precious from doing the big sins that would embarrass me.

One or two parent seminars a year will not fix motivations that shallow. But fifteen hours a week can give the youth pastor time to:

1. Partner with the other pastors to deepen parents' walk with Jesus.
2. Call out and teach parents how to lead spiritually at home.
3. Equip them to parent biblically.
4. Partner with other pastors to introduce lost parents to Jesus.

Part One of this book unpacks the extensive biblical material that identifies parents as the primary spiritual leader in the life of a teenager. In addition, the three chapters in that section will present biblical passages that speak to deepening parents' walk with Jesus, teaching parents how to spiritually lead, and equipping them to parent biblically. Then, current studies will provide secondary support for these approaches.

Immersing Every Teenager in the Full Life and Ministry of the Congregation

Teenagers who only connect with peers and a few youth leaders generally will not walk in faith in adulthood. Those who spend their teenage years with multiple heart connections with believers of all ages—and those who serve King Jesus with believers of all ages—probably will. That fact is sobering given the high percentage of teenagers who spend their teenage years living in a youth ministry bubble at church.

> Most teenagers who leave high school
> with little love for the Bride eventually
> will wander away from the Groom.

Dan Dupee says to Christian parents:

> Strong families are the starting point, but not the ending point. The ending point is the body of Christ, since "from whom the whole body, being fitted and held together by what every joint supplies, according to the proper working of each individual part, causes the growth of the body for the building up of itself in love" (Ephesians 4:16). Your kids need to see that other respectable grown-ups are as crazy about Jesus as their parents.[68]

---

[68] Dan Dupee, *It's Not Too Late* (Grand Rapids, MI: Baker Books, 2016), 109.

In both the Old and New Testaments, God's people usually appear in intergenerational relationships. "O God, You have taught me from my youth, and I still declare your wondrous deeds. And even when I am old and gray, O God, do not forsake me, until I declare your strength to this generation, your power to all who are to come" (Psalm 71:17–18).

Youth pastors need to do fresh thinking about ways churches can use buildings, budgets, and calendars to create rich webs of relationships around every child, teenager, and adult. One result might be young adults who love Christ's church and who consider the full congregation to be family. Dupee adds, "It lends power and credibility to the gospel message when ... children see it embraced by people for whom they have affection and respect and who they know are genuinely interested not only in Jesus but in them."[69]

A youth ministry book that has sparked conversation is Chap Clark's *Adoptive Youth Ministry*. He makes a strong case for teenagers and members of the congregation adopting each other. Clark believes teenagers have much to give as well as receive, so he calls for mutual adoption.

Paul is the only New Testament writer to use the term *adoption* (*huiothesia*). God the Father adopts believers into His eternal family, and He intends for these "siblings" to live in warm unity. Even more importantly, He intends for the generations to link arms and serve the Kingdom of Christ together.

A youth pastor might ask teenagers,

1. "Not counting relatives and youth workers, how many adults in our church know your name, know interesting things about you, and often show interest in your life?"
2. "Not counting relatives, how many children in our church would say you are important to them relationally and spiritually?"

---

[69]Ibid., 110.

A youth pastor could dramatically change the answers to those questions by spending fifteen hours a week:

1. Multiplying mutual adoptions between teenagers and all ages of believers.
2. Calling out and equipping every teenager to take places of Kingdom service with children or adults.

Churches can temporarily build attendance by keeping teenagers in the youth bubble and by allowing entertainment to overshadow service and ministry. (After all, for fifty years we have conditioned teenagers to embrace fun and peers.) But the research is irrefutable. Such an approach will lead to a high percentage of those "great crowds" walking away from the church after high school. Who would call that successful youth ministry? Youth ministry authority Walt Mueller says:

> It's ironic that one of the marks of today's emerging generations is a deep need for community and connectedness, and yet we plan and program in ways that cut them off from experiencing community and connectedness with people who aren't their own age. It's also ironic that while we say we want to see our kids embrace Jesus and mature into a deep faith that's integrated into all of life, we separate them from the wisest and most seasoned members of the body.[70]

Part Two of this book provides specific guidance regarding the building of heart connections between teenagers and all the generations of the congregation. That section also presents specific ways that teenagers can be mobilized to perform the functions of the church (evangelism, worship, discipleship, ministry, and community) while linking arms with all the generations. That

---

[70] Walt Mueller, "Why Youth Ministry Shouldn't Be the Greatest Show on Earth," June 1, 2017, cpyu.org.

accelerates Kingdom impact now and builds lifetime disciples for the future.

Leading Traditional Youth Ministry

Grade-schoolers need to search Scripture to find how to imitate Jesus on a recess playground. Senior adults need to search the Word to discover new ways to be on mission after retirement. Age-specific ministry is a valuable part of church life.

Mark Cannister notes, "There is a strong consensus among intergenerational specialists that while the church embraces intergenerational values, it is also essential to maintain important age-specific ministries."[71] The research project reported in the book *Why They Stay* found that "a young adult who attended a church with a ministry to students was more likely to have stayed as an adult, and one who attended a church without a ministry to students was more likely to have strayed."[72]

Part Three of this book provides specific guidance regarding ministry with teenagers making up a youth group. That section also presents specific ways that teenagers can be mobilized to perform the functions of the church (evangelism, worship, discipleship, ministry, and community) while linking arms with their peers and youth leaders.

Churches should celebrate:

1. The youth pastor who presents text-driven talks that are relevant to the specific issues of the teenage years.
2. Open-group Bible study that presents foundational concepts to all teenagers.
3. Intensive discipleship for those specific teenagers who have made a clear decision to follow Jesus.

---

[71] Mark Cannister, *Teenagers Matter: Making Student Ministry a Priority in the Church* (Grand Rapids, MI: Baker Academic, 2013), 139.
[72] Steve R. Parr and Tom Crites, *Why They Stay: Helping Parents and Church Leaders Make Investments That Keep Children and Teens Connected to the Church for a Lifetime* (Bloomington, IN: WestBow Press, 2015), 105.

4. Groups of teenagers who move out to evangelize and make disciples locally and globally.
5. Teenagers doing things that are fun. Warm friendships and laughter are part of what King Jesus was promising in John 10:10.

Ministry built around thirds still provides time for youth worship, open-group Bible study, intensive discipleship, evangelistic and caring outreach, and fellowship. Time is also well-spent on a few special youth events, but only those that are strategic to creating lifetime disciples. Programming that does not contribute to lifetime faith has to go away.

The Motivation for Ministry in Thirds

Gratitude and adoration toward King Jesus provide the motivation for youth ministry. Veteran youth leader Rodger Nishioka says, "The doctrine of grace serves as a key theological basis for youth ministry because [teenagers], more than people at any other age, desperately need to know they are loved for who they are without ties to performance or condition."[73]

Grace flows from the Gospel. Pastor and author J.D. Greear puts it this way:

> The gospel is that Christ has suffered the full wrath of God for my sin. ... Second Corinthians 5:21 says that He actually became my sin so that I could literally become His righteousness. ... When I receive that grace in repentance and faith, full acceptance becomes mine. ... That means that God could not love me any more than He does right now, because God could not

---

[73] Rodger Nishioka, "Theological Foundation for Youth Ministry: Grace" in *Starting Right: Thinking Theologically about Youth Ministry*, ed. Kenda Dean, Chap Clark, and Dave Rahn (Grand Rapids, MI: Zondervan, 2001), 249.

love and accept Christ any more than He does, and God sees me in Christ.[74]

Romans 5:18–19 says: "So then as through one transgression there resulted condemnation to all men, even so through one act of righteousness there resulted justification of life to all men. For as through the one man's disobedience the many were made sinners, even so through the obedience of the One the many will be made righteous."

When teenagers grasp this, the discovery will be life-changing for them. Young followers of Christ often have a hard time understanding forgiveness, typically because it has not been modeled at home, and thus live with shame. Leaders might teach them that God sees them in Christ and then ask: "When God looks at His Son, how much sin does He see? When God looks at you in His Son, how much sin does He see?"

For teenagers, grasping grace will lead to gratitude. Nishioka says, "Grace is completely unexpected. There is no logic and no reason as to why God, who is the maker of the universe, should love us so incredibly that God would send Jesus to die for us."[75]

Swindoll explains the results of grace when he says:

> All who embrace grace become "free indeed." Free from what? Free from oneself. Free from guilt and shame. Free from the damnable impulses I couldn't stop when I was in bondage to sin. Free from the tyranny of others' opinions, expectations, demands. And free to what? Free to obey. Free to love. Free to forgive others as well as myself. ... Free to serve and glorify Christ.[76]

---

[74] J.D. Greear, *Gospel: Recovering the Power that Made Christianity Revolutionary* (Nashville, TN: B&H Publishing Group, 2011), 46–47.
[75] Nishioka, *Starting Right*, 246.
[76] Charles R. Swindoll, *Grace Awakening* (Nashville, TN: Thomas Nelson, 2003), 40–41.

What motivates teenagers toward such obedience? Greear says:

> Those people who get better are those who understand that God's approval of them is not dependent on their getting better. ... Abiding in Jesus will produce all of the fruits of the Spirit in you—but not by having you concentrate particularly on any of those things. You concentrate on Jesus. You rest in His love and acceptance, given to you not because of what you have earned, but because of what He has earned for you.[77]

Perhaps all this helps youth leaders envision a ministry filled with believers grateful for grace and hearts full of adoration toward their King. Swindoll says:

> Fortunately, grim, frowning, joyless saints in Scripture are conspicuous by their absence. Instead, the examples I find are of adventurous, risk-taking, enthusiastic, and authentic believers whose joy was contagious even in times of painful trial. ... The contrast between then and now is staggering. The difference, I am convinced, is grace.[78]

Grace-filled relationships within the body of Christ are wonderful, but they are not the end of the story. David Platt lifts eyes to the bigger picture when he says, "Enjoy his grace and extend his glory. This is the twofold purpose behind the creation of the human race. ... God blesses his people with extravagant grace so they might extend his extravagant glory to all people of the earth."[79]

---

[77]Greear, *Gospel*, 14.
[78]Swindoll, *Grace Awakening*, 279.
[79]David Platt, *Radical* (Colorado Springs, CO: Multnomah Press, 2010), 65, 69.

The Big Picture

The diagram on page 72 illustrates youth ministry in thirds. The terms that make up this diagram deserve careful consideration.

The Power of the Holy Spirit

Jesus said: "Abide in Me, and I in you. As the branch cannot bear fruit of itself unless it abides in the vine, so neither can you unless you abide in Me. I am the vine, you are the branches; he who abides in Me and I in him, he bears much fruit, for apart from Me *you can do nothing*" (John 15:4-5, emphasis added).

The Functions of the Church

Many individuals, churches, and groups have similar views of the five functions of the local church. Many believers would embrace the following definitions:

> **Worship**—Worship is any activity in which believers experience God in a meaningful, spiritually transforming way. Encountering God in worship transforms us more and more into His likeness.[80]
>
> **Evangelism**—Evangelism is believers sharing the Gospel with lost persons. Evangelism is asking them to repent of their sins, to put their faith in Christ for the forgiveness of sins and the free gift of eternal life, and to follow Him forever as Lord. Evangelism is the good news spoken by believers and lived out in their lives.
>
> **Discipleship**—Discipleship is a process that begins after conversion and continues throughout a believer's life. Discipleship occurs when one believer engages

---

[80] Gene Mims, *Kingdom Principles for Church Growth* (Nashville, TN: LifeWay Christian Resources, 1994), 34-57.

YOUTH MINISTRY THAT LASTS A LIFETIME

POWER OF THE HOLY SPIRIT →

ARENAS
- Teens and the Congregation
- Teens and the Youth Group
- Teens in Families

FUNCTIONS
- WORSHIP
- EVANGELISM
- DISCIPLESHIP
- MINISTRY
- COMMUNITY

RESULTS
- GLORY OF GOD
- LOVE GOD
- LOVE PEOPLE
- MAKE DISCIPLES OF ALL NATIONS

another and the result is that both become more Christlike in what they think and do.

Ministry—Ministry is meeting another person's need in the name of Jesus. Ministry grows out of a transformed and serving life. Ministry is the normal function of every believer.

Community (or Fellowship)—Community is person-to-person relationships. Churches tend to have the kind of fellowship they want and our Lord expects when they focus on evangelism, discipleship, ministry, and worship.

The Results

God intends that the functions of the church (and individuals and families) will lead to the fulfillment of the Great Commandment and the Great Commission. In other words, He intends that the church will:

- Love God.
- Love people.
- Make disciples of all nations.

The Great Commandment is taken from Matthew 22:35-39: "One of them, a lawyer, asked Him a question, testing Him, 'Teacher, which is the great commandment in the Law?' And He said to him, 'You shall love the Lord your God with all your heart, and with all your soul, and with all your mind.' This is the great and foremost commandment. The second is like it, 'You shall love your neighbor as yourself.'"

The Great Commission is taken from Matthew 28:18-20, "And Jesus came up and spoke to them, saying, 'All authority has been given to Me in heaven and on earth. Go therefore and make disciples of all the nations, baptizing them in the name of the

Father and the Son and the Holy Spirit, teaching them to observe all that I commanded you; and lo, I am with you always, even to the end of the age.'"

The Ultimate Outcome

A Christ-follower exists for the glory of God. A family exists for the glory of God. A youth ministry and a church exist for the glory of God. God's Word is crystal clear (emphasis added):

- "Therefore, having been justified by faith, we have peace with God through our Lord Jesus Christ, through whom also we have obtained our introduction by faith into this grace in which we stand; and we exult in hope of *the glory of God*" (Romans 5:1-2).
- "Whether, then, you eat or drink or whatever you do, do all to *the glory of God*" (1 Corinthians 10:31).
- "For all things are for your sakes, so that the grace which is spreading to more and more people may cause the giving of thanks to abound to *the glory of God*" (2 Corinthians 4:15).
- "For this reason also, God highly exalted Him, and bestowed on Him the name which is above every name, so that at the name of Jesus every knee will bow, of those who are in heaven and on earth and under the earth, and that every tongue will confess that Jesus Christ is Lord, to *the glory of God* the Father" (Philippians 2:9-11).

Guiding the Church toward Youth Ministry in Thirds

Of course, a youth pastor who implements youth ministry in thirds on his own will soon be unemployed. Well-meaning senior pastors, church leaders, parents, and even teenagers think they are "paying" the youth pastor to provide programming for teenagers.

Period. Without preparation, youth pastors could face parents who go ballistic when they think they are losing their babysitting service. And the teenagers may only see this as trading the Xboxes for "old people who smell weird."

Slow and careful change seems much wiser. Movement in new directions might follow this flow:

1. The senior pastor, youth pastor, and core church leaders pour over Scripture, pray deeply, and draft a direction for the future.
2. That group invites leadership staff, core parents, core leaders, core teenagers, and core congregation members to speak into, adjust, and then affirm the direction.
3. Leaders present the plan to the full church and youth group.
4. The church creates ongoing ways to celebrate, affirm, and tangibly reward the youth pastor as he takes the lead in new directions.

For a much fuller discussion concerning making these changes, see the book *Growing Young: Six Essential Strategies to Help Young People Discover and Love Your Church* by Kara Powell, Jake Mulder, and Brad Griffin.

As noted before, the great majority of our youth pastors love King Jesus supremely, embrace their calling fully, and do their work tirelessly. But by doing those things the church expects them to do, the great majority of church teenagers are not becoming world-changing disciples as adults.

> Everyone knows the definition of *insanity*.
> Clearly the time to move toward change is now.

Top Ten Factors Leading to a Lifetime Faith and Love for the Church

A lifetime of study of Scripture, digesting research, and observing high school graduates leads this author to humbly suggest the top ten most important factors in developing a lifetime faith. The list presupposes a relationship with Jesus.

1. A teenager who shares a warm heart connection with a parent who is transparent about his adoration of God's Son, who embraces God's written Word, and who lives for the glory of God.
2. A teenager who shares a life-on-life relationship with a discipler who adores Jesus and guides the teenager through a challenging, systematic discipleship process.
3. A teenager who shares heart connections with many members of the congregation and who shares a mutual "adoption" with one or more adults who adore Jesus.
4. A teenager who actively serves and ministers with other generations as well as with peers.
5. A teenager who actively participates in intergenerational worship on Sunday mornings.
6. A teenager who knows how to correctly interpret Scripture and to pray, and who takes responsibility for his own spiritual growth.
7. A teenager confident about having conversations that are evangelistic or that call for a reasoned defense of the faith.
8. A teenager who knows how to apply the principles of Scripture to his life while navigating a pluralistic culture.

9. A teenager who approaches vocation and all of life with a sense of divine calling and an appreciation for his spiritual gifts.
10. A teenager connected to significant adults who welcome and work together on doubts and questions.

PART 1

Ministry with Teenagers and Their Families

Chapter 6

Biblical Parenting

By Richard Ross

... bring them up in the discipline and instruction of the Lord.
—Ephesians 6:4

The Spiritual Leadership of Parents

Biblically sound youth pastors acknowledge that God's *primary* plan for moving the faith down through the generations is the home. Those youth pastors know God's *primary* plan for getting truth into the lives of teenagers is at the feet of their parents.

> "We will not conceal them from their children, but tell to the generation to come the praises of the Lord, and His strength and His wondrous works that He has done. For He established a testimony in Jacob and appointed a law in Israel, which He commanded our fathers that they should teach them to their children, that the generation to come might know, even the children yet to be born, that they may arise and tell them to their children, that they should put their confidence in God and not forget the works of God, but keep His commandments" (Psalm 78:4-7).

> "Train up a child in the way he should go, even when he is old he will not depart from it" (Proverbs 22:6).

"Fathers, do not provoke your children to anger, but bring them up in the discipline and instruction of the Lord" (Ephesians 6:4).

Fathers and Mothers

Since the time of Moses, faithful Jews have quoted the words of the first commandment, the *Shema*, each morning and evening. No passage in the Old Testament is held in higher regard. Jesus declared that this was the greatest commandment (Matthew 22:35-38). Therefore, one would expect the words that immediately follow the *Shema* to be of great importance:

> "Hear, O Israel! The Lord is our God, the Lord is one! You shall love the Lord your God with all your heart and with all your soul and with all your might. These words, which I am commanding you today, shall be on your heart. You shall teach them diligently to your sons and shall talk of them when you sit in your house and when you walk by the way and when you lie down and when you rise up" (Deuteronomy 6:4-7).

God declared the primary commandment and then immediately declared the primary means of perpetuating that commandment through the centuries—parents teaching their own children. James Hamilton provides an explanation of crucial Hebrew words:

> The Hebrew verbs rendered "you shall repeat" and "you shall talk" are second person masculine singular forms. Unlike English, which does not distinguish between masculine and feminine forms of the second person pronoun "you," Hebrew has a masculine form for "you" and a feminine form for "you." The fact that these forms are masculine singular means that, as Moses addressed the nation of Israel, he directed the responsibility to teach the "sons" toward the fathers.

The fact that the form is singular urges the conclusion that Moses did not give this responsibility to some abstract group of fathers in the community but to each individual father. It does not take a village, it takes a father.[81]

Later, God inspired Solomon to present the crucial role of mothers to assist in the spiritual instruction of children: "Hear, my son, your father's instruction and do not forsake your mother's teaching" (Proverbs 1:8). Similar passages are found in Proverbs 6:20, 31:1, and 31:26.

In Proverbs, the teaching of the mother is placed side by side with the teaching of the father. It shows us the importance the Bible places on the mother's teaching and the fact that both parents must be believers in order to bring up the children in the faith. ... The book of Proverbs honours the role of women more than the role given them either in ancient society or in many cases modern society by placing their teaching in the home alongside that of the father.[82]

Parents Take First Position

Parents who want to see their children bring great glory to God:

- Have a deep appreciation for pastors and church leaders who impact their teenagers.
- Work aggressively to deepen relationships between their children and those church leaders.

---

[81]James Hamilton in, Randy Stinson and Timothy Paul Jones, eds., *Trained in the Fear of God: Family Ministry in Theological, Historical, and Practical Perspective* (Grand Rapids, MI: Kregel Publishers, 2011), 37.
[82]Peter J. Gentry, "Raising Children, the Christian Way" *The Journal of Discipleship and Family Ministry* 2.2. (2012): 96-109.

- Build family schedules around the ministries and services of the church.
- Become firm supporters of all the church is doing to spiritually impact their teenagers.

But at the same time, parents never abdicate to the church the final responsibility for the spiritual instruction of their teenagers. Kingdom parents do not need research to convince them that spiritual leadership in the home is vital.

- They honor God in their home because He is the sovereign Lord of the universe.
- They joyfully accept His authority because they revere Him, love Him, and have hearts of gratitude toward Him.
- They embrace His principles of parenting and family life because He is God and because they know His precepts offer the only hope for a healthy family.

Research

Parents choose how to lead at home based on the Bible, not on research or pragmatic concerns. At the same time, it is at least interesting when studies support the concept that parents are the primary influencers of their children.

- "The majority of U.S. teenagers seem basically content to follow the faith of their families with little questioning. When it comes to religion, they are quite happy to go along and get along. The popular images of 'storm and stress,' 'Generation Gap,' and 'teen rebellion' may describe the religious orientations and experiences of most teenagers of prior generations. But they do not accurately portray the religious realities of most teenagers in the U.S. today."[83]

---

[83] Smith with Denton, *Soul Searching*, 120.

- "The evidence clearly shows that the single most important social influence on the religious and spiritual lives of adolescents is their parents. Grandparents and other relatives, mentors, and youth workers can be very influential as well. But normally parents are most important in forming their children's religious and spiritual lives."[84]
- "All research indicates that the most significant influence on the life of the teenager comes from parents. It is only when parents become uninvolved that their role of guidance is replaced by the gang, the peer group, or the friend at school."[85]
- "Though a child may be strongly influenced by his or her friends, the power of this peer group emerges as dominant only when the relationship of love with parents is vastly diminished. Caring parents are the primary influence in shaping the moral values of their children."[86]

Parents do not make just a little bit more of a difference but a great deal more of a difference. This fact has been documented by Christian Smith, Kenda Dean, Kara Powell, Jim Burns, Mark DeVries, David Kinnaman, Rob Rienow, Brian Haynes, Mark Holman, and a host of other researchers and writers.

Youth pastors and leaders who proclaim publically and privately that parents have the primary role in the spiritual lives of their teenagers are on a firm biblical foundation. Youth pastors and leaders who work toward making parents heroes in the eyes of their teenagers are as well. Youth ministries that do not call out, equip, and support parents to take first position do not have a biblical footing.

---

[84]Ibid., 56.
[85]Gary Chapman, *The Five Love Languages of Teenagers* (Chicago, IL: Northfield Publishing: 2000), 12.
[86]Merton P. Strommen and Richard A. Hardel, *Passing On the Faith: A Radical New Model for Youth and Family Ministry* (Minnesota: Saint Mary's Press, 2000), 85.

Parents Support the Church

The home is the primary location for the spiritual development of a teenager. Family teaching and modeling are the primary tools for that development. Even though the church is second to the home in importance, the church still is indispensable. The King has decreed believers are to assemble (Hebrews 10:25). Youth pastors call families who honor and obey Him to do just that.

Beyond just attending, parents support and serve in the church. They do so because they adore their King and live under His reign. At the same time, parents can celebrate the fact that their faithful service makes it more likely that their children will walk in faith for a lifetime. That is exactly what leaders observed in a recent study:

> The important thing to note here is that young adults remember the roles their parents played in church, whether they participated or refrained from involvement. It made an impression on them. They remember that their parents held important leadership positions and demonstrated commitment and spiritual maturity. The people who stayed in church had parents who were "all in."[87]

In addition to other church roles, wise parents can support youth ministry by:

1. Serving on a Parent Advisory Council (see chapter 17).
2. Teaching or discipling teenagers (see chapter 13).
3. Serving on a Youth Ministry Lead Team (see chapter 17).
4. Sponsoring events, providing their homes, or providing logistical support.

---

[87] Parr and Crites, *Why They Stay*, 115.

The Sabbath

Youth pastors call parents and teenagers who embrace the supremacy of Christ to take seriously the fourth of the Ten Commandments: "Remember the sabbath day, to keep it holy" (Exodus 20:8). They are just as focused on obeying that commandment as they are on those forbidding adultery and murder.

> If parents allow a teenager to skip worship on Sunday morning to participate in some activity or competition, they have communicated their true priorities to the teenager.

The same is true if parents allow a teenager to take a job that requires Sunday work or they allow him to sleep in after a hard week. Those actions and decisions will make a more lasting impression than what parents try to teach about priorities.

If Christian parents would take a clear stand against allowing their children to participate in activities on Sunday morning, most leagues and other competitions would have no choice but to move to other days and times. At the very least, parents and teenagers need to communicate to leaders at the very beginning that they will be faithful to team obligations—except Sunday participation.

Relationships at Church

Whether the youth pastor and church leaders are people of influence with a teenager depends in large measure on relationships. Relationships depend on consistency. If a teenager is inconsistent in church and youth group involvement, relationships likely will be weak and influence diminished.

A teenager beginning to protest going to church may not be rebellious. He may be revealing that relationships there are becoming so weak they do not draw him there. Teenagers live so much in the present that it does not take many scattered absences from church for them to begin feeling distant from leaders and even peers. A teenager's complaints about attending Sundays may be the logical consequence of family decisions to miss now and then.

Parents who make church life a family priority are much more likely to see their children in heart connections with leaders of influence there. They also are likely to see those children equally committed to a local church during college days.

Disciple Parents

Parents occupy the position of primary spiritual leader in the home, but that does not mean all parents are sufficiently discipled and transformed for that task.

- **Some church parents desire of their child:** "Be successful so I can feel pride."
- **Discipled parents desire:** "Live for the glory of God, regardless of the cost or sacrifice."

- **Some church parents desire of their child:** "Be happy so I can be happy."
- **Discipled parents desire:** "Think and act as Jesus, as revealed in Scripture."

- **Some church parents desire of their child:** "Be moral so you don't embarrass me."
- **Discipled parents desire:** "Complete your unique purpose as you join King Jesus in bringing His Kingdom on earth."

- **Some church parents believe:** "God exists for me. He intends that I have a successful, prosperous life."
- **Discipled parents believe:** "God exists. The entire created order exists for His glory, including my family and me."

- **Some church parents believe:** "God's highest priority is my happiness and my family's happiness."
- **Discipled parents believe:** "We are redeemed to be restored to a relationship with God, to die to self, and then to live out God's unique plan for our lives."

- **Some church parents believe:** "My family and I follow many of the rules of our religion because it makes our lives turn out better."
- **Discipled parents believe:** "Conformity to Christ is motivated by joyful adoration of His greatness and gratitude for the Gospel."

Concrete Steps toward Discipling Parents

The youth pastor can link arms with the other pastors to:

1. Walk every baptized church member back through his or her salvation experience.

Most have only a vague memory that, "Somebody told me to bow my head and repeat a little prayer." Parents need to consider, "Do I believe that Christ is God, died for my sins, and thus is my only hope for forgiveness? Have I genuinely repented of my sin? Will I accept the invitation of Jesus to die to myself and become His disciple?"

Some informed church leaders believe at least *half* of church members are lost people. That would have to include many very nice, very moral parents.

2. Make whatever change in church schedule is necessary to get most genuine Christ-followers, including parents, into a discipleship group that is:

- Very small—following the model of Jesus with Peter, James, and John.

- Comprehensive—with a curriculum designed to cover all the key topics in discipleship.
- Accountable—with very open sharing and grace-filled accountability.
- Single-gender—because of the depth of sharing and accountability.
- Transforming—filled with the spiritual disciplines.

3. Start a small group/Sunday School class for parents.
This would not be a parenting class specifically but would follow the same curriculum as the other classes and groups. A class or group composed of parents of teenagers can become a support for those parents. They can become a "cord of three strands" that is not easily broken (Ecclesiastes 4:12). They also can target some of their prayers toward their own teenagers, the youth ministry of the church, and this generation of teenagers.

The group can approach any passage of Scripture in the curriculum from the unique perspective of parents. Three questions always can be part of the conversation:

- Is there a truth here I can live out in new ways before my children?
- Is there a truth here that can help shape how I am parenting?
- What are ways I can build this truth into the hearts of my children?

A Bible study group for parents will be more valuable if it includes:

- Honest sharing and mutual support ("Guys, I have to be honest. I really blew it with my son last week.") ("I

couldn't believe it. I read some Scripture to my kids, and they were actually interested.")
- Prayers that involve everyone and include adoration of the King, prayer over Kingdom issues, warm intercession over one another's families, and prayer that Christ be glorified through illness or healing.

Mostly Who Parents *Are* Is Who Teenagers Will *Become*

The more spiritually vibrant and alive the parents are, the more this will overflow into their children. And the more transparent parents are about their own spiritual journey, the more their teenagers will tend to follow in similar directions.

Everyone enjoys a good movie based on a best-selling novel. Here is an analogy. The Bible is the book—the "novel." The "movie" based on the Bible is the daily lives of parents. Parents have the great privilege and the great responsibility to unfold for their children the intriguing drama of real life in Christ. They turn the truth of Scripture into high-definition "video" that is easy for their children to see and absorb (1 Corinthians 11:1).

Teenagers are influenced by seeing parents in church every Sunday. They are even more influenced when they see that public faith lived out in the privacy of the home. Rob Rienow notes, "Our character, on display at home, is literally constructing our children's framework for understanding who God is. This is happening in a powerful way through whatever takes place daily in our homes."[88]

Church leaders determine what they want teenagers to be by the time they are 18. Then they spiritually develop parents into that image. Youth pastors champion spiritually alive parents because that is *the* most powerful way to develop spiritually alive teenagers.

---

[88]Rob Rienow, *Visionary Parenting* (Nashville, TN: Randall House, 2009), 39.

> Perhaps the most powerful thing church leaders can do
> to give teenagers a lifetime faith
> is to stimulate *parents'* spiritual pilgrimage.
> Now that is a new paradigm.

Teach Parents How to Parent

Parents of infants and parents of college students need specific training in parenting. As children grow, parents find themselves parenting every age of child for the first time. Without specific training, most parents tend to reproduce the failed parenting approaches their own parents may have used. Youth pastors need to partner with church leaders in designing training events that provide instruction in both parenting and spiritual leadership.

Parents Who Connect with the Hearts of Children

One primary goal of parent training involves teaching parents how to parent in a way that deepens relationships. Parents who keep heart connections (relationships) warm and strong usually see visible evidence that their faith and values are passing to their children.

Rob Rienow says, "When the hearts of fathers (and mothers) are fully engaged with their children, and the hearts of children are turned to their parents, everyone's heart is prepared to receive the love of Father God expressed through His Son Jesus."[89]

Spiritual impact flows from one generation to the next through a relational pipeline. Parents who keep that heart connection warm and strong usually see visible evidence that their faith and values are passing to their children.

The Old Testament ends, "Behold, I am going to send you Elijah the prophet before the coming of the great and terrible day of the Lord. He will restore the hearts of the fathers to their children

---

[89] Rob Rienow, *Five Reasons for Spiritual Apathy in Teens* (Nashville, TN: Randall House, 2015), 14.

and the hearts of the children to their fathers, so that I will not come and smite the land with a curse" (Malachi 4:5-6). God intended that the preaching of the Gospel, symbolized by John the Baptist (the prophesied Elijah), would lead many to salvation. Only in that new life in Christ would parents and children form the deepest of heart connections.

Too little quality time together can damage heart connections. If a parent and teenager grow distant from each other, the pipe is pulled loose. The probability is that the parent then will have little spiritual impact, even if the parent teaches and lives out biblical truth before the teenager.

Parents who try to discipline with shouting and angry tirades damage heart connections. Angry outbursts do not permanently improve teenage behavior; they only weaken heart connections and thus weaken parental influence. Biblically sound parents follow the example of Father God. Just as He did at Mount Sinai, parents announce the boundaries of behavior (commandments) and the rewards (blessings) and punishments (curses) that immediately will follow obedient or disobedient behavior.

If a teenager loses a heart connection with parents, he or she often will try to fill the void by giving the pipe to peers. Some of those peers, from weak homes, may fill the pipe with faithlessness and confused values. But even then Christ offers hope for healing and restored relationships. Parents rebuild heart connections by:

Forgiving teenagers for pain they have caused.

- Asking them for forgiveness as appropriate.
- Moving away from emotional outbursts toward teens.
- Spending focused time together.

Parents Who Build Up and Bless Teenagers

Teenagers tend to embrace the faith of parents who genuinely communicate their significance, provide believable encouragement, and daily say, "I love you." Even during the teen years, the most powerful words teenagers ever hear come from their parents.

Sadly, some Christian parents communicate that they never are completely satisfied with what their teenager does. Their teenager may have come to believe he or she can never please the parent. The teenager could be pushing away the parent's faith only because the teenager finally gave up trying to please the parent. Wise and godly parents:

- Major on majors.
- Avoid constant criticism.
- Build up and encourage.
- Say "I love you" often.

Overextending in Extracurricular Activities

Extracurricular activities should build emotionally and spiritually vibrant children and teenagers. When extracurricular activities take so much time that they make time with parents and family impossible, then they no longer are accomplishing their purpose. Just because being on one team is good does not mean being on three teams is better. Parents who push their children to overextend in activities need to ask themselves hard questions:

- Am I pushing my child to overextend in hopes he will excel—because I need to prop up my weak self-concept by living vicariously through the successes of the child?
- Am I pushing my child to overextend in hopes that he will win a major scholarship and thus allow me to hold on to college savings?

Parents need to consider these critical questions:

- Has your family's schedule become so crazy that too few minutes are available for focused attention on children, quiet conversations, and even spiritual leadership?

- If your answer is "yes," will you take a ruthless inventory to discover what is pulling family members apart evenings and weekends?
- Once you discover what is causing the craziness in schedules, will you ask for God's leadership in knowing what changes must be made?

Parents Investing in Other Teenagers

Parents can make an eternal impact in the lives of teenagers from other homes. Church leaders can present these challenges to parents:

- You can share the good news of Christ with children and teenagers who do not yet know Him. You might say your home feels like Grand Central Station with children coming and going. Watch for conversations that can turn toward Christ.
- You can ensure teenagers who do not yet know Christ are welcomed and valued when the youth group gathers at your church. You can speak truth to parents who would push such teenagers away.
- You can assist with supervision when the youth group gathers to ensure that including teenagers who do not yet know Christ does not change the personality of the group.
- You informally can share truth with young believers who come under your roof.
- You can allow the Christian atmosphere of your home to make a lifetime impression on those who never see such a model. You can become intentional about letting others observe truth lived out in home relationships.
- You can help fill the emotional emptiness of children and teenagers who receive little love, affirmation, or focused attention in their own homes.

- You can become a prayer warrior for the teenagers who come to your home—in some cases becoming the *only* person who is bringing a child's name before Christ.
- In short, you can see your home as a primary mission field and an expression of your personal call to ministry.

Chapter 7

Families and the Five Functions of the Church

By Richard Ross and Hyeungyong Bak

As for me and my house, we will serve the Lord.
—Joshua 24:15

The end goal of family ministry is not families sitting on the couch singing "Kumbaya." The end goal is families making disciples, locally and globally, for the glory of God. That also is the end goal of the entire church. Spiritual practices in the home and more transformed family members are valuable because they prepare the saints for Kingdom service.

The Current Situation

Youth pastors who think faith talks are common in church families would be mistaken. According to research from Kara Powell, only one in eight teenagers talks about faith with Mom, and even fewer talk with Dad.[90]

The great majority of church parents now believe that taxi driving is their part in the discipling of their children. They believe their role is to drive children to church to be discipled by professionals. Fewer than 10 percent of born-again families read the Bible together during a typical week or pray together apart from mealtime.[91]

---

[90] Kara Powell, Brad Griffin, and Cheryl Crawford, *Sticky Faith* (Grand Rapids, MI: Zondervan, 2011), 118.
[91] George Barna, *Revolutionary Parenting* (Carol Stream, IL: Tyndale, 2007), 31.

Parental leadership was very different in the biblical period. In Jewish history, at least until the mid-first century A.D., family education was perceived primarily as the father's responsibility.[92] Even though synagogues were regarded as the place for studying the Hebrew Scriptures, the home still remained the primary place of children's learning.[93]

Rob Rienow adds,

> We fail to realize that Sunday school and youth groups did not exist until the late 1800s. For the first nineteen centuries of Christianity it was understood that parents were called by God to disciple their children, and that the home was the primary place for this to happen.[94]

Biblically sound youth pastors and church leaders call parents to lead their families to perform the functions of the church for the glory of God. Such activity matters for the Kingdom today, and it makes lifetime faith more likely for teenagers. A study of many congregations found that "the ministries having the greatest success at seeing young people emerge into mature Christians, rather than contented churchgoers, are those that facilitate a parent-church partnership focused on instilling specific spiritual beliefs and practices in a child's life from a very early age."[95]

According to Mike McGarry, "Parents should view themselves as their children's 'first pastors,' while simultaneously inviting other church family members to codisciple their children."[96] Jonathan Edwards said, "Every Christian family ought to be as it were a

---

[92]O.M. Bakke, *When Children Became People* (Philadelphia, PA: Fortress, 2005), 176.
[93]Timothy Paul Jones, ed., *Perspectives on Family Ministry: 3 Views* (Nashville, TN: Holman Bible Publishers, 2009), 18.
[94]Rienow, *Visionary Parenting*, 96.
[95]George Barna, "Spiritual Progress Hard to Find in 2003," December 22, 2003, barna.org.
[96]Cole and Nielson, *Gospel-Centered Youth Ministry*, 93.

little church, consecrated to Christ, and wholly influenced and governed by His rules. And family education and order are some of the chief means of grace. If these fail, all other means are likely to prove ineffectual."[97]

Parents who increasingly love Jesus supremely, exude Jesus, talk about Jesus, connect with the hearts of their kids like Jesus, and shape those hearts like Jesus likely will see their adult children:

- Join glorious King Jesus in bringing His Kingdom on earth, in the power of the Spirit.
- Make disciples who make disciples among all peoples, down through the generations.
- Multiply worshipers before the throne forever.

Worship

Most family prayer and conversations about faith are spontaneous, but some take place at planned times. Some call these planned times "family worship," and others call them "faith talks." They reflect the words from Deuteronomy 6:7, "when you sit in your house." Each family should follow Christ's leadership to know how often to gather for worship. Families just beginning this practice might begin by gathering weekly.

Such times usually include longer prayer, worship and praise, and reading and discussing Scripture. The place of Bible teaching in family worship will be addressed in the next section of this chapter.

Family prayer must be a part of spiritual instruction. Prayer during family worship will seem more natural if parents pray with their children every night.

---

[97]Jonathan Edwards, "Farewell Sermon," accessed September 19, 2016, sermonaudio.com.

> Almost *every* believing parent
> prays with a toddler at bedtime.
> And almost *none* with a teenager.
> Who needs it more?

Prayer during family times must have variety. Too much predictable sameness makes prayer seem like a ritual. Parents and teenagers need to think of new ways to pray, new places to pray, and new words in prayer.

Family prayers should include prayer for one another. Sometimes, parents may find it meaningful to stand behind children with hands on their shoulders or head while they pray over them. Children can do just the same over parents and siblings.

As with any prayer group, families should be faithful in recording their prayers of intercession so later they can record the ways God chose to answer. Such journaling teaches children a life-altering lesson about the power of prayer.

Spiritual instruction in the home lacks power without prayer. Most of the prayers parents will pray over their children will be closet prayers. Some concerns only can be expressed in private. But the complement to closet prayers are those prayers children get to hear.

- Children and teenagers need to hear Kingdom parents interceding to God for them.
- They need to hear the depth of their parents' love revealed in those prayers.
- They need to hear how keenly their parents want to see impact radiating out from their lives.
- They need to hear their parents release them to God's call and purposes. Hearing such prayers may be one of the most important experiences a child can have.

Parents pray with their children "when you lie down and when you rise up" (Deuteronomy 6:7). Parents open the Bible and teach their teenagers how to pray. Parents complement teaching times by actually praying out loud with their sons and daughters. Over time, parents will see their prayers reflected in the prayers of their offspring. Parents who model well will:

- Hear more spiritual maturity in their teenager's prayers.
- Hear their teenager asking to be filled by the Holy Spirit of God.
- Hear their teenager praying more and more prayers of praise and adoration before asking for anything.
- Hear requests move from a focus on "me and mine" to a focus on the glory of God.
- Hear their teenager pray for Christ's Kingdom to come on earth in the midst of hard situations, rather than just automatically asking that all hard situations go away.

Children growing up praying about global Kingdom issues are very likely to become Kingdom-focused young adults. Wise parents include prayer for the nations and for Kingdom concerns when the family gathers for study and worship. Wise youth pastors provide printed and internet sources for fresh prayer needs locally and globally.

Discipleship

Dan Dupee observes, "We cannot assume that our time of spiritual influence ends when our kids become teens. On the contrary, parents routinely discover years after the fact that a specific conversation or example had a lasting impact."[98]

As reported in chapter 6, parents are the most important influence in the lives of their teenagers, for good or ill. Youth pastors assist believing parents in making that a positive, Kingdom-shaping influence. John Revell points out:

---

[98]Dupee, *Not Too Late*, 65.

In Deuteronomy 6:6, after issuing what Jesus recognized as the greatest commandment, Moses instructed the people to keep God's command in their hearts. But in verse 7 he added: "Impress them on your children." The original Hebrew word translated impress was used of a person carving a message into stone with a hammer and chisel. God used graphic imagery to communicate the need for fathers to imbed these truths in the minds of their children.[99]

Mothers have an important role in spiritual leadership at home. But according to Scripture, God's normative plan calls for fathers to stand in first position. Ephesians 6:4 states, "Fathers, do not provoke your children to anger, but bring them up in the discipline and instruction of the Lord." Related to that passage, Revell adds:

> [The] Lord placed the responsibility for discipling children squarely on the fathers. In the minds of first century readers the word "discipline" encompassed the broad concept of education. It went beyond mere verbal instruction to include loving correction and punishment, with the long-term goal of shaping the child. The word "instruction" included verbal instruction, admonishment, warning, and correction. When connected to the final phrase "of the Lord," we see the father is expected to provide the broad-based, long-term biblical and spiritual training essential for molding a child in the ways of the Lord.[100]

Parents are in a battle for the hearts and minds of their children. The voices that would confuse their kids are loud and often have hours a week to communicate their messages. Even in the best of

---

[99]John Revell, "As You Are Going, Make Disciples—Starting in the Home!" June 2001, sbclife.net.
[100]Ibid.

situations, parents have too few minutes to confront those voices. Therefore, parents must never allow busy schedules to keep them from gathering the family for warm, Spirit-empowered Bible teaching as part of family worship.

Family ministry pioneer Rob Rienow notes, "God believes in discipleship small groups ... He just has another name for them. He calls them families."[101] Youth pastors often are experts related to small groups. They can train parents how to involve teenagers in planning the sessions and making them interactive. Dads or single moms can lead their "small group" in interesting discussions from Scripture built around:

- What the parent is learning from his own daily time in God's Word (since the overflow of a parent's spiritual life is valuable to children).
- A printed guide the youth pastor or other church leaders have placed in parents' hands.
- What parents learned from last Sunday's sermon or adult Bible study group.

Parents use family Bible study time to assist their children in forming a God-centered worldview. Another term for *worldview* is "a philosophy of life."

"We define world view as the underlying belief system held by an individual that determines his/her attitudes and actions about life."[102] Every person has such a belief system.

The following three statements could not be more central to parenting:

- "A person's concept of reality and truth determines his beliefs!"
- "A person's beliefs shape his values!"

---

[101] Rienow, *Visionary Parenting*, 9.
[102] Glen Schultz, *Kingdom Education* (Nashville, TN: LifeWay Press, 2002), 38.

- "A person's values drive his actions!"[103]

Parents must teach the Bible to their teenagers in a way that affirms Scripture as absolute truth. Powerful voices consistently tell teenagers that:

- All truth is relative.
- Being sincere is more important than being right.
- Respecting others means accepting whatever they believe as the truth.
- Many ways exist to know God, and they all are equally valid.

Parents can be grateful for any assistance the church is giving in teaching a God-centered worldview to their children. But at the same time, parents cannot abdicate to the church the final responsibility for ensuring this is done.

As another tool of discipleship, parents must create opportunities for family members to share spiritual testimonies. Tom Elliff reminds parents:

> One day it will be impossible for your friends and family members to access all that is stored up in the library of your heart. That is why it is imperative for you to share with them now the simple story of your conversion. A legacy of faith in Christ is the most important thing you can leave with them. So, tell them "your story." And, while you're at it, ask them about theirs.[104]

Beyond their story of conversion, parents need to tell their children what God has been teaching them lately. They need

---

[103]Ibid., 46.
[104]Tom Elliff, "First-Person: Has Your Family Heard Your Testimony?" January 10, 2003, bpnews.net.

to describe ways they are growing as a follower of Jesus. Youth pastors can ask parents, "How many days, months, or years has it been since you said to your child,

- 'Come sit down over here. I want to share with you something new that King Jesus is doing in my life right now.'
- 'I have been looking forward to breakfast this morning, because I want to tell you what the Holy Spirit showed me in Scripture during my quiet time early this morning.'
- 'The truth of that sermon hit me hard this morning. Son, you need to know what I committed to God at the close of the service.'"

Parents' past and present testimony will shape a Kingdom generation. The absence of such words will stunt the next generation. The same is true regarding a parent's living testimony and example. Dan Dupee reminds parents:

> When we live with integrity—when our faith is real and shows up on the field of play on Saturday as it will in church on Sunday—then our kids can experience the most powerful teaching tool we have: our example. If instead we have a faith that exists only in the "religious" realms of our lives, our kids are likely to be at best confused and at worst disillusioned.[105]

Evangelism and Ministry

Parents are not responsible for the decisions their children make about receiving or rejecting a relationship with Jesus Christ. Every person young or old stands before God on that issue. Children

---
[105] Dupee, *Not Too Late*, 72.

reared in warm, godly homes with full knowledge of salvation can choose to reject the Savior. But parents *are* responsible for parenting and communicating in a way most likely to lead to the conversion of each of their children. The stakes could not be higher.

- No parental duty matters more than introducing one's children to Jesus Christ.
- Parents who do not teach what Scripture says about salvation almost guarantee their children will simply make up their own ideas.
- Children who make up and trust their own ideas about salvation likely never will be saved.
- Children from Christian homes who never are saved spend eternity in hell.
- Children more easily grasp the grace of God when they live with parents who relate to them in grace.
- Praying for the salvation of children is the highest privilege and gravest responsibility of a parent.

Evangelistic Families

A teenager's closest circle of friends should be growing Christians. The older children become, the more powerful the influence of that inner circle becomes. This same principle applies to those teenagers they date or court. They must be maturing Christians or harm usually will follow.

Parents who desire to rear Kingdom children will lead them to first have a heart for lost people near at hand. Christian teenagers in firm relationships with an inner circle of other Christ-followers can safely reach out to lost peers. In essence, those believing friends become a rescue squad—holding onto and supporting one another as they reach across the quicksand to friends who need Jesus.

Some church parents fearful of the world try to isolate their children from the lost. Those same parents probably hope their children will grow up to be strong adults who then will try to win the world to Jesus. Unfortunately, there is no magic switch a parent can throw to change an older teen's mindset from "avoid lost people at all costs" to "draw all people to Christ." Parents who have reared the family with a bunker mentality probably will get young adults content to live out their lives in that bunker.

On the other hand, children who cannot remember a time when family members were not focused on lost friends and acquaintances will probably grow into young adults with hearts for the world. Hearts for their "Jerusalem" will lead easily to a concern for the "uttermost parts of the earth." Youth pastors gently can ask parents:

- How many days or years has it been since you joined with your child to pray by name for a lost friend?
- Which acquaintance of your child could you volunteer to help your child pick up for church this Sunday or Wednesday?
- Could your children name an adult friend of yours they know you are seeking to lead to Christ?
- When was the last time someone made a profession of faith that a member of your family had a part in reaching?
- What is a step you can take this week to lead members of your family to have hearts for the lost?

Compassion Ministries

Youth families can take steps to serve others in Christ's name. When families engage in serving others on a regular basis, teenagers form permanent memories that what matters most is not themselves, but Christ and His mission of redemptive love to others. Youth ministry professor Justin Buchanan and his wife Sarah challenge families to:

> ... make note of the needs that exist right where you are, and you can lead your family and your teenagers to specifically begin meeting those needs in the name of Jesus. Are there homeless, jobless, widows, orphans,

elderly, refugees, addicts, special needs, or others you can seek in order to display the Gospel by meeting their needs and sharing the hope of Christ?[106]

Church adult groups and the youth group may perform compassion ministries. Even if that is true, there still is great value in caring for others as a family. Performing acts of service with the family may be one of the most powerful discipling experiences any child or teenager can have.

Missional Families

God is calling families to missions locally, nationally, and globally. Parents may need to partner with the youth pastor or other leaders to become knowledgeable about opportunities for their family in each arena.

Serving Thanksgiving dinner at the rescue mission or traveling to a Third World country can be powerful steps moving an entire family toward the supremacy of Christ. The subject of family mission trips will be addressed in detail in the following chapter.

Parents Releasing Teenagers to Missions

In addition to family missions involvement, youth pastors challenge parents to call out, equip, and send out their own children for the sake of the harvest. Victor and Esther Flores draw from the words of Jim Elliott to ask,

> Remember how the Psalmist described children? He said that they were as an heritage from the Lord, and that every man should be happy who had his quiver full of them. And what is a quiver full of but arrows? And what are arrows for but to shoot? So, with the strong arms of prayer, draw the bowstring back and

---

[106]Justin Buchanan and Sarah Buchanan, "Raising Teenagers to Live on Mission for God" in *Everyday Parenting*, ed. Alex Sibley (Fort Worth, TX: Seminary Hill Press, 2017), 111.

let the arrows fly—all of them, straight at the Enemy's hosts.[107]

Organizations that send teenagers on international mission trips (or challenging domestic trips) report that parents can be obstacles. Often those organizations discover teenagers eager to go but parents unwilling to release them. To those parents, Victor and Esther say, "When our arrow-children are sent out to local or foreign mission fields, we must be willing to sacrifice our small, temporal, self-advancing dreams for our children so that our King's eternal gospel-advancing mission can be realized all over the world."[108]

Any discussion of releasing children to missions raises concerns for their safety. Parents have a responsibility to ensure that their teenager will serve with an agency or organization that has taken every prudent measure to ensure the safety of young missionaries. And, parents have a responsibility to teach their children how to minimize risks away from home.

But in the end, godly parents must place the lives of their children in the hands of the Father—just as they did in the delivery room. Parents who live for the glory of God must release their children to risk and even martyrdom if sovereign God should so ordain.

Nothing is more important than the family's role in taking the Gospel to those who do not know Christ. The Great Commission propels out families to their neighborhood, state, nation, and world. Spiritually alive families exist to see every person on the block, in the high school, and around the world hear about Jesus.

---

[107] Victor Flores with Esther Flores, *Raise to Release: A Missional Mandate for Parents* (Houston, TX: Lucid Books, 2015), 134.
[108] Ibid., 18.

Community

Biblically sound youth pastors pray for, plan for, and work toward relational closeness in the homes of all their teenagers. Of course, they want families to find happiness in this sense of community. But there are Kingdom implications beyond just happiness. Tim Kimmel reports, "The goal of the church's family ministry is to connect to the heart of each individual family leader in such a way that it better prepares those parents to develop a heart connection to their kids that subsequently inclines those kids towards a deeper love for the Lord and kindness toward others."[109]

Perhaps the greatest threat to community in the home is busyness. Many church parents honestly believe they do not have the time available to better connect with their children. But they may be mistaken.

The average middle-aged adult watches television two hours and forty minutes per day.[110] Online activities are on top of that. Perhaps parents have more discretionary time than they realize. If parents watched one hour of television an evening, suddenly one hundred minutes would be available for family worship, supervising homework projects, crafting wise discipline, and listening to the hearts of children. A family will not reach its potential as a Christ-focused family without managing media.

Church events designed to bring parents and teenagers together can deepen relationships and thus lead to more closeness when families are at home. Many of those types of events are described in the next chapter.

---

[109] Tim Kimmel, *Connecting Church and Home* (Nashville, TN: Randall House, 2013), 23.
[110] The Nielsen Company, "Cross-Platform Report," accessed February 9, 2017, nielsen.com.

Conclusion

God's plan for parenting goes beyond an individual parent and teenager. God is orchestrating entire generations. Just as God desired for generations of Hebrews to bless the nations, God still desires that parents join Him in moving the Christian faith down through all the generations for His grand purposes.

Parents spiritually lead the family because they want God's best for their teenager. But they should also lead out because they someday want their adult child to spiritually lead their grandchild—and for their grandchild to someday spiritually lead their great-grandchild.

Rob Rienow says to parents,

> It is easy to become so focused on getting through the day at hand that we seldom consider the big picture of God's calling for parents and grandparents. You have been invited into a multigenerational mission. God created your family to be a discipleship center that will build a legacy of faith for generations to come.[111]

---

[111]Rienow, *Visionary Parenting*, 17.

Chapter 8

Programming to Impact Families
By Richard Ross

That the generation to come might know, even the children yet to be born, that they may arise and tell them to their children, that they should put their confidence in God.
—Psalm 78:6-7a

Wise youth pastors sense that they can see more lifetime disciples when they commit a third of their ministry time to impacting families. For financially supported youth pastors, that might represent fifteen hours a week. This chapter presents some of the most strategic ways those hours can be invested.

Training Parents to Spiritually Lead at Home

Most parents of teenagers did not grow up with parents who were intentional about spiritual leadership in the home. Consequently, those parents cannot easily visualize what that would look like.

Parents do not like to look foolish in front of their children. If parents have not been leading spiritually at home, they will be reticent to take steps in that direction—even if leaders convince them they should. Parents need practice in order to feel comfortable and confident about leading spiritual practices at home. Youth pastors and other church leaders should *demonstrate* to parents what that looks like.

For example, leaders need to illustrate what family worship can look like with various ages of children and teenagers. A few pieces of furniture can create a living room set, and a family (with some coaching beforehand) can demonstrate how to share leadership with the teenagers, make the Bible interesting, and pray creatively.

Also, six chairs can be positioned as a minivan on its way to soccer practice. A family can demonstrate how to have an unplanned spiritual conversation "as you walk by the way." Parents watching demonstrations may tend to say, "Now I get it. I feel pretty confident I can do that."

These three steps will build confidence:

1. First, leaders should show parents how to lead with skits involving families on stage.
2. Then, leaders should let all parents practice through role plays involving only adults.
3. Then, when parents are showing some confidence, leaders should bring together all the actual families to explore spiritual disciplines and practices in a safe environment at church.

These three steps make it much more likely that parents will actually begin to lead spiritually at home. At minimum, such training should be provided once a year.

Parenting Seminars

Monthly Seminars

As children grow, parents find themselves parenting every age of child for the first time. Youth pastors need to partner with church leaders in designing training events that provide instruction in parenting.

Ron Hunter, founder of the D6 family ministry movement says, "D6 finds value with placing parents with other parents whose oldest children are at similar seasons of life thus allowing proper applications relevant to life. ... The church leadership and people within small groups provide insight, experience, and understanding."[112]

Leaders who are serious about moving parents to first position with their children will move toward assembling parents monthly during the school year. Meeting less may mean far too many issues will not receive attention. Church leaders and parents can plan gatherings to address such issues as:

- Biblical discipline that shapes the heart.
- Sexual purity for a lifetime.
- The influence of friends.
- Understanding youth culture.
- The dark side of the online world.
- Students and vocational direction.
- Bringing your family schedule under control.
- The impact of your marriage on children.
- Normal and dangerous signs in your teenager's behavior.
- Transitions to middle school, high school, and college.
- Honoring rites of passage.
- Creative ways to worship as a family.
- Sharing truth in the flow of family life.
- Teaching your teenager new ways to pray.
- Local, U.S., and global missions opportunities for families.
- Ideas for making family Bible study transformational.
- Passing the spiritual disciplines to your children.
- How to communicate with your teenager.
- Practical ways parents can support youth ministry.
- Preparing your teenager for short-term missions.
- When true love doesn't wait.
- Alcohol and other drugs.
- Preparing your teenager for college.

---

[112]Ron Hunter, "The D6 View of Youth Ministry," *Youth Ministry in the 21st Century: Five Views*, Chap Clark, ed. (Grand Rapids, MI: Baker Academic, 2015), Kindle version.

A mega-church might invest a thousand dollars in a gathering for hundreds of parents on one of these topics. A very small church might only invest encouragement as three parents gather to sharpen one another with their insights, to support one another by linking arms, and to strengthen one another through prayer. Both gatherings can be valuable.

The weakest parents in the church tend to attend only on Sunday morning. They seldom return to church the other six days. Moving some parent gatherings to Sunday morning opens the possibility of involving the parents who most need help.

Parent Gatherings That Run Several Weeks

Monthly gatherings are targeted to the largest possible attendance of parents. On the other hand, a study that runs several weeks usually will involve fewer parents. At the same time, a multi-week study offers broader and longer-lasting change. Usually a multi-week study will involve a curriculum, book, or video resource.

Family Mission Trips

Yearly or more often, families who love Jesus can go with Him on mission trips. Parents may need to partner with the youth pastor and other church leaders to become knowledgeable about opportunities for the family.

- Parents can consider arranging family finances in order to take a family mission trip in the U.S. or internationally—either their family alone or with other families.
- Parents can consider giving one day of a typical family vacation to do something of Kingdom importance (feed people in the name of Christ, paint a ministry building, etc.).

Family mission trips nationally and globally require money. God may be calling families to choose to live more frugally than necessary in order to release unusual funds for the glory of Christ. Some years, an international mission trip as a family may take priority over the newest entertainment technology.

In addition to U.S. and international mission trips, families also can be involved in missions close to home. Possibilities include such ministries as:

- Work on homes owned by those with no resources.
- Nursing home services.
- Assisting at a shelter (homeless, refugee resettlement, abuse).
- Backyard Bible clubs.

Parents Conducting Rite of Passage Ceremonies

Wise youth pastors assist parents in providing the Christian equivalent of a Bar/Bat Mitzvah near a teenager's thirteenth birthday.[113] Most families will remember this ceremony for a lifetime. For the Jewish family, the ceremony means the child, at the age of 13, is deemed ready for religious responsibility. He or she becomes a "Son/Daughter of the Covenant."

For the Christian youth, this is a time when a young person assumes responsibility for spiritual disciplines. He begins to understand the transition that is taking place in his life as Scripture characterizes: "When I was a child, I used to speak like a child, think like a child, reason like a child; when I became a man, I did away with childish things" (1 Corinthians 13:11).

The Christian Bar Mitzvah can be planned on the eve of the thirteenth birthday. Or, it might be planned for the evening before the child enters junior high or middle school. Or, it might be planned for the evening before the child promotes into the youth ministry of the church.

---

[113]Bar is for boys and Bat is for girls.

Consider Christian Teenagers with Lost Parents

Christian families can provide a ceremony for Christian teenagers whose lost parents will not provide such an occasion. Elements should be added to the ceremony that affirm the significance of the child's actual parents and call for obedience and honor to them.

Preparation

In preparation for this very special time:

1. *Consider purchasing or making a lasting symbol of the event to present to the young person.* For example, one family purchased a real sword to present to a son. The father used the sword as part of the charge that he gave his son during the ceremony. The sword now is displayed in a place of honor in the son's bedroom and may well become a valued heirloom passed to his children someday.
2. *Make a decision about how parents will participate.* In homes with a Christian father, the father may take the lead with the ceremony. Single mothers should take the lead in their homes and should take all the assignments in the ceremony directed to parents. The same is true for single fathers.

    In homes with a father who has not been converted, parents need to discuss in private what his role will be. Some non-Christian fathers may feel comfortable reading some or all of the assignments in the ceremony for fathers. Others may want to attend but have their wives do all the speaking. Still others may not want to be present for the ceremony. Though this will be a cause for sadness, Christian mothers should move forward with providing a memorable ceremony for the teenager. In the days that follow, the mother may want to invite

Christian men to provide spiritual leadership for her children.

3. *Turn off every kind of phone.* This is one of those moments that must be protected from any kind of interruption.

The Ceremony

Jewish families have the advantage of many centuries of tradition in the conducting of Bar and Bat Mitzvahs. There is no official Christian equivalent. Each family must find its own way in planning one. Here is a buffet of options families can consider.

1. *Court of Honor*—Invite several key adults chosen by the youth. Each adult presents a charge, gives a blessing, and then presents a remembrance gift of that blessing.
2. *The Blessings of the Father and the Mother*—Kingdom parents bless (affirm and encourage) their children. They give careful thought to the words they will use.
3. *The Charge of Names*—Parents review the meaning of the family name through research online. They present to the child the positive traits and traditions of the family name. They review those in previous generations or the present extended family who have been people of honor.

    Parents read aloud Philippians 2:5-11. They present the meaning of that Name and present a charge to bring honor rather than dishonor to that Name.
4. *The Altar of Isaac*—Parents might borrow a six-foot table from the church and cover it with a sheet. They ask their son or daughter to lie on the table with arms folded. Both parents stand near the table and read words similar to the following:

Mother: "We do not own you. You are the Lord's. We will not hold you so tightly that you miss God's plans and purposes for you. We will seek in every way to protect you, unless that ever becomes contrary to God's call on your life. If His clear call should involve sacrifice or risk, we will not stand in the way but will cheer you on."

Father: "We will surrender our will for you to God's divine will, regardless of the cost or inconvenience to us. We will cast a vision before you of God's special plan for His glory and His plan to reach the nations of the world. We will teach you basic biblical doctrines, stewardship, and service. We will pray each day for your impact on culture and the world for God's glory."[114]

Parents present to their child a signed copy of what mother and father have just said.

Intergenerational Family Experiences at Church

When families get out of the car on Sunday mornings, they generally will not be all together again until they arrive back at the car to go home. Most church programming divides age groups into silos (separate age-group compartments). Some age-specific programming makes perfect sense, but an overbalance may harm spiritual impact.

Parents need to provide full support for education and ministries that are targeted to specific age groups of children and youth. Parents also need to champion church experiences that bring families together. Here are several possibilities:

---

[114]Covenant adapted from Mark Matlock, *Generation Hope* (Friendswood, TX: Baxter Press, 2002).

Family Retreats or Camps

- Dinner together by families—with suggested discussion topics.
- Prayer together by families.
- Divide by sexes to answer questions and then combine to compare answers.
- One session for parents and a separate session for children or teenagers.
- Time together in father/daughter and mother/son pairs.
- Experience team-building challenges by families.
- Use a campfire service for family members to affirm one another.

Parent Appreciation Banquets

- Children or teenagers purchase tickets with their own money for parents.
- Children or teenagers prepare the food and decorate according to the theme.
- Children or teenagers wait on tables and present entertainment.

Family Fellowships

- Cookouts.
- Sports, baseball, etc.
- Son/father and mother/daughter events.
- Messy games.
- Scavenger hunt.
- Family-wed game (similar to the Newlywed Game).
- Role playing, while dressed as the other generation.
- "Oscars" awards show—Best Family Vacation, etc.

How should parents and leaders feel when moving in these directions and some teenagers ask, "What could be worse than a retreat with parents?" Leaders should remember a dysfunctional culture has had sixty years to say to teenagers it is best to live surrounded by friends and distant from adults. Leaders cannot expect teenagers to change their thinking overnight.

The quickest way to change their thinking is to create a reputation for quality whenever families gather. Soon teenagers will be saying, "I thought the retreat was going to be so lame, but it was a blast! The games were the best we ever had, and I loved the late-night prayers. To be honest, I never really knew my dad's prayers were so deep."

Choosing Family or Age-Specific Programming

Some youth pastors are nervous about moving in these directions. They wonder if doing so will lead to critical voices that say: "We hired you to take care of our kids. Why are you doing things for families instead of your real job?"

Senior pastors need to take the lead in moving the church toward a stronger focus on families. This includes turning the hearts of the congregation in that direction. And it includes leading the decision-making structures of the church to affirm those changes. Then age-group pastors can make changes in their work without putting themselves at risk.

The youth pastor and his core planning team continually need to ask this question: "Considering the ministry objective before us at this moment, will we be better served to provide a program/event for teenagers and their leaders or teenagers and their families?" In the most biblically sound, family-focused church, the answer some of the time will be a program/event for teenagers and their leaders.

But positive change in youth ministry will lead to far more family events than has been common in the past. That is because those specific events seem to have a better chance of leading teenagers toward lifetime faith and Kingdom impact. That is true for teenagers in intact families and for spiritual "orphans" whom church families "adopt" every time there is a family activity on the calendar.

Resources

The pastors of a church might ask, "How much does our church spend on God's 'Plan B' for discipleship and spiritual transformation? In other words, how much does the church spend preparing to teach the Bible on church property? What are we investing in printed resources, bringing in trainers for our teachers, building educational buildings, and providing teaching supplies?"

Then the pastors might ask, "How much does our church spend on God's 'Plan A' for discipleship and spiritual transformation? In other words, what budget funds do we invest to prepare parents to spiritually lead their own children? How many times this past year have we gathered parents to inspire and train them to teach the things of God to their children? What resources have we placed in their hands to assist them?"

Many pastors discover they are spending ten or twenty times more to disciple children at church than at home. To verbalize "Our church champions parents as spiritual leaders" is easy. But making systemic changes in the budget to support that vision is more valuable.

The Youth Pastor

The following youth pastors are much more likely to impact families and to see far more teenagers walk in faith for a lifetime:

1. Youth pastors who partner with other pastors to reach lost parents.
2. Youth pastors who speak positively about parents and families before the youth group and the

congregation. They make clear to all that they respect parents and their role.
3. Youth pastors who know the names of parents and which family members go together.
4. Youth pastors who minister to parents during times of crisis.
5. Youth pastors who return phone calls, emails, and text messages from parents the day they arrive. Youth pastors who follow through with promises.
6. Youth pastors who teach parents all they know about youth culture, how teenagers see the world, and how teenagers are growing. Youth pastors who become more and more knowledgeable in these fields so they will have more to share with parents.
7. Youth pastors who become more and more knowledgeable about how parents think, how biblical families function, and how parents should parent. Regardless of their marriage/family situation, they let parents know they are becoming increasingly competent in these disciplines.
8. Youth pastors who show respect to parents who come with a concern. They listen carefully without becoming defensive. They develop a reputation for being approachable.
9. Youth pastors who give parents clear ways to help set the strategic direction of the youth ministry and ways to join teams that implement programs and events.
10. Youth pastors who communicate youth ministry plans to all parents well ahead of time.
11. Youth pastors who consistently plan ways for parents and teenagers to build stronger heart connections with one another.

Programming to Impact Families

12. Youth pastors who keep families focused on the overarching goal of glorifying God by proclaiming Jesus as Lord in the power of the Spirit.

Youth pastors who link arms with other church leaders can see observable growth and change in families. Such transformation can lead to:

- Teenagers who love Christ with all their heart, soul, mind, and strength.
- Teenagers who adore the King above relationships, possessions, comfort, and a long life.
- Teenagers who absolutely would lay those things down at Christ's command.
- Teenagers who are not bound to the culture.

A generation such as that can—quite literally—change the world.

PART 2

Ministry with Teenagers as Part of the Congregation

Chapter 9

Biblical Relationships in the Congregation
By Richard Ross

*The glory which You have given Me I have given to them,
that they may be one, just as We are one.*
—John 17:22

Just use your imagination. One of your teenagers has graduated and has just started his freshman year at college in another state. The first Sunday morning has arrived. Asleep in the dorm, he hears his phone alarm go off at 7:00 a.m. Will he get up and find a new church or roll over and sleep until noon?

Lots of variables will shape that decision, but high on the list is the answer to this question: Whom, primarily, does the freshman love? If his greatest love is for his high school youth pastor, he may go back to sleep—since the youth pastor is many miles away. If his greatest love is for the old youth group, he may go back to sleep—since the youth group also is many miles away. But if his greatest love is Jesus, expressed through the full congregation, he may get up—ready to find another expression of the church he has grown to love.

The Current Situation

When teenagers are asked to speak at church, they often speak of their love for the youth group and seldom speak of their love for the church. They often speak of their love for their Christian friends and seldom speak of their love for the congregation. Things do not look promising for their walk of faith in young adulthood.

It all comes down to this central question: Are teenagers more likely to develop a lifetime faith, embracing the full supremacy of Christ…

- …when they primarily relate to a handful of youth leaders and experience church almost exclusively with people their same age?
- …or when they build heart connections with many significant adults in their lives and experience church in a rich web of intergenerational relationships?

Youth pastor and author Mark Howard says:

> Fostering community within the youth group cannot be an entirely separate endeavor from cultivating the youth's participation within the wider church. Our failure on this point may be one of the primary reasons why so many youth walk away from church life once they go to college: they never really felt a part of the corporate church community in the first place; they only felt a part of the youth group.[115]

Rob Rienow now is a leader in the family ministry movement. But for years, he was a youth pastor. He wisely discovered the value in connecting his youth group to the full church. He reports that:

> One of the things I had to repent of as a youth pastor was working so hard to win the hearts of students to the youth group. I wanted the youth group to be the place where they found their connection, community, and identity. What I should have done was sought to win their hearts to their families and to our entire church. My mission should have been to help them find their connection, community, and identity

---

[115]Cole and Nielson, *Gospel-Centered*, 82.

at home and with our entire church family, not only with their peers.[116]

Unfortunately, the awareness that Rienow came to as a youth pastor is not the norm. Youth ministry professor Duffy Robbins reports:

> We have unwittingly cultivated a congregational environment in which teenagers are being cut off from the very adult relationships that can sustain them through the turbulence of the adolescent years, and teach them about mature Christian faith. We are, in effect, nurturing in teenagers an appetite for youth group (from which they will eventually graduate), while weaning them from involvement in the life of the broader church that can sustain their spiritual growth as adults.[117]

After conducting the National Study of Youth and Religion, Christian Smith concluded, "Teenagers ... are structurally disconnected from the adult world. ... But in terms of the implications of our work for churches, the two key words are engagement and relationships. It can't just be programs or classes. ... Real change happens in relationships, and that takes active engagement."[118]

Scott Wilcher cuts right to the chase when he says that "if we fail to connect students to the adult church, we undermine their faith development."[119] Unfortunately, relationships across the generations are not the norm in churches today. Kinnaman observes that "many churches have allowed themselves to become

---

[116]Rob Rienow, *Limited Church: Unlimited Kingdom* (Nashville, TN: Randall House, 2013), 260.

[117]Duffy Robbins, *Building a Youth Ministry That Builds Disciples* (Grand Rapids, MI: Zondervan, 2011), 102.

[118]Katelyn Beaty, "Lost in Transition." *Christianity Today*, 53 (10), 34.

[119]Scott Wilcher, *The Orphaned Generation: The Father's Heart for Connecting Youth and Young Adults to Your Church* (Chesapeake, VA: UpStream Project, 2010), 166.

internally segregated by age ... and, in doing so, unintentionally contribute to the rising tide of alienation that defines our times."[120]

Youth pastors keep their vision both on the present and on the future. They can be pleased when they hear their current teenagers love the youth group. But at the same time, youth pastors ask themselves, "Will these same people love the church and walk in faith when they are 25 or 35?"

Biblical Support

Chap Clark finds strong biblical support for church as an intergenerational family:

> The New Testament writers apply this family metaphor, consistently encouraging believers to see one another as brothers and sisters. In Galatians 6:10, we are admonished to "do good to all people, especially to those who belong to the family of believers" and Hebrews 2:11 claims that Jesus "is not ashamed" to refer to His followers as His "brothers and sisters."[121]

The entire Bible pictures the people of God living, worshiping, and serving in such intergenerational relationships:

- "One generation shall praise Your works to another, and shall declare Your mighty acts" (Psalms 145:4).
- "Both young men and virgins; old men and children. Let them praise the name of the Lord, for His name alone is exalted; His glory is above earth and heaven" (Psalm 148:12–13).

---

[120]Kinnaman, *You Lost Me*, 203.
[121]Chap Clark, ed., "The Adoption Model of Youth Ministry," *Youth Ministry in the 21st Century: Five Views* (Grand Rapids, MI: Baker Academic, 2015), Kindle version.

- "Blow a trumpet in Zion, consecrate a fast, proclaim a solemn assembly, gather the people, sanctify the congregation, assemble the elders, gather the children and the nursing infants. Let the bridegroom come out of his room and the bride out of her bridal chamber" (Joel 2:15–16).
- "So we, who are many, are one body in Christ, and individually members one of another" (Romans 12:5).
- "For all of you who were baptized into Christ have clothed yourselves with Christ. There is neither Jew nor Greek, there is neither slave nor free man, there is neither male nor female; for you are *all one* in Christ Jesus" (Galatians 3:27–28, emphasis added).

According to Clark:

> In traditional youth ministry, we may use the rhetoric of community to describe our practices, and we believe that what we do actually is an expression of Christian community (although limited to peers and a handful of adults), but generally the best we offer is a shallow and generationally limited approximation of what the New Testament treats as normative.[122]

Jesus said, "Permit the children to come to Me" (Mark 10:14). Concerning that passage, Rob Rienow says, "Notice Jesus was not married, nor did He have children. Jesus set the example for every believer, regardless of their family situation, to intentionally nurture faith in children, and participate in God's multi-generational Great Commission. We are all called to 'next generation' ministry."[123]

Timothy Paul Jones adds:

> Whenever I preach Deuteronomy 6, I almost always take people to the words of Jesus in Matthew 12:48 or

---
[122]Ibid.
[123]Rienow, *Limited Church: Unlimited Kingdom*, 176.

to Paul's words in 1 Timothy 1:2, pointing out to them that—in the New Covenant—a role that was limited to parents in the Old Covenant becomes God's call to the entire church in the New Covenant, to become the parents-in-faith for every younger believer. In the New Covenant, Deuteronomy 6 becomes a call to the whole community.[124]

The declaration of every older adult should be Psalm 71:17–18: "O God, You have taught me from my youth, and I still declare your wondrous deeds. And even when I am old and gray, O God, do not forsake me, until I declare your strength to this generation, your power to all who are to come."

Observations

Leaders should shape youth ministry based on the truth of Scripture alone. Because of God's brilliance, His Word is all that is necessary to create ministry designs that lead to lifetime faith. Careful observers of churches and youth ministries report what we already know from Scripture. Those with biblical, intergenerational relationships do, indeed, create believers with stronger faith.

> **Kara Powell**: "Specifically, churches with close intergenerational relationships show higher faith maturity and vibrancy."[125]

> **Chap Clark**: "Transformation happens most deeply in the lives of teenagers when they are engaged in the broader life of the church and connected to a network of caring adults. ... By being fully connected to, embraced by, and included in the historic body of

---

[124]Timothy Paul Jones, personal correspondence with the author.
[125]Powell, Mulder, and Griffin, *Growing Young*, 173.

Christ, adolescents can safely and securely transition into and become healthy adult believers."[126]

Mark Cannister: "Nothing is more reflective of healthy student ministries than students who launch into the full and robust life of the church. In order for this to happen, though, the broader church must be prepared for and committed to receiving teenagers into its midst by valuing them for who they are and allowing them to contribute to the whole life of the church."[127]

Dave Rahn: "When responsible adult leaders enter into the lives of students, they can help students take initial steps toward new levels of responsibility and self-reliance. Because the chief way students learn is through modeling others (usually Christian adults), it's important that adults are caring enough to inspire and show the way for students."[128]

David Kinnaman: "The Christian community is one of the few places on earth where those who represent the full scope of human life, literally from the cradle to the grave, come together with a singular motive and mission. ... Flourishing intergenerational relationships should distinguish the church from other cultural institutions."[129]

Christian Smith: "While Smith has identified several factors that contribute to high levels of faith

---

[126] Chap Clark, *Adoptive Youth Ministry: Integrating Emerging Generations into the Family of Faith* (Grand Rapids, MI: Baker Academic, 2016), 137, 38.
[127] Cannister, *Teenagers Matter*, 117.
[128] Dave Rahn and Terry Linhart, *Evangelism Remixed: Empowering Students for Courageous and Contagious Faith* (Grand Rapids, MI: Zondervan, 2009), 64.
[129] Kinnaman, *You Lost Me*, 203.

among emerging adults, personal relationships with adults (parents and other caring adults) who connect teenagers to the faith community in the middle and high school years is necessary in almost all cases."[130]

Lisa Pearce and Melinda Lundquist Denton: "[They] found that teenagers who were the most committed to their faith reported that, in addition to having parents and close friends who shared their beliefs, they were also connected to a faith community that provided 'a welcoming, challenging atmosphere that values and integrates youth.'"[131]

Culture Intensifies the Need

Teenage culture became an appendage to mainstream society for completely dysfunctional reasons. During the last half of the twentieth century, parents who became consumed with their own issues mostly abandoned the young. Teenagers grasped one another for survival. It was *Lord of the Flies*. When the young figured out the adults mostly were gone, they had to build some sort of culture, even if it was filled with danger.

Somehow the church looked at that pathological development and decided it would be a dandy pattern for the church to follow. So for sixty years, teenagers mostly have experienced church with people their same age. The youth group is almost an appendage to the congregation.

Tim Elmore reports that teenagers today spend about sixty hours a week with peers and about sixteen hours with adults.[132] For most of human history, the reverse of this was true.

Culture expert Walt Mueller says:

---

[130] Cannister, *Teenagers Matter*, 117.
[131] Ibid.
[132] Tim Elmore, presentation at Southwestern Seminary, April 6, 2013.

We need the security of a place to live with and be loved by others: home. Today's emerging generations are no different. They long for a place to belong and to call home. For many, their yearning is amplified by the fact that broken family situations and the lack of healthy peer relationships have left them with a huge relational void. They want connections, relationships, and community.[133]

Every teenager needs adult relationships in the church. This is even truer for teenagers who have been abandoned by parents or other key adults. Chap Clark notes that "communities must make sure that each student has a few adult advocates who know and care for him or her. ... It takes several consistently supportive and encouraging messages to counteract the effects of systemic abandonment."[134]

Scott Wilcher observes, "They ... hope someone older and wiser will teach them how to be an adult, that someone will care enough to see their need for spiritual parenting, and get close enough to see the potential in them to be unlikely but powerful heroes for the Kingdom."[135]

An increasing percentage of teenagers in most churches have parents who do not know Christ. All the research says they almost are destined to leave the church in late high school or certainly after graduation. They are dangling by a thread.

Barring an outright miracle, their only hope for a lifetime faith is multiple heart connections with spiritually alive adults who hold to them tenaciously. If those teenagers are not drawn routinely into the full church family, sirens should be going off and warning lights flashing.

---

[133] Walt Mueller, *Engaging the Soul of Youth Culture* (Downers Grove, IL: InterVarsity Press, 2006), 192–93.
[134] Chap Clark, *Hurt 2.0: Inside the World of Today's Teenagers Youth, Family, and Culture* (Grand Rapids, MI: Baker Academic, 2011), 202.
[135] Wilcher, *Orphaned Generation*, 92.

Teenagers today go along and support church youth programs as long as there is a momentary payoff, such as fun trips, glitzy youth centers, and more time with peers. As teenagers develop new interests and begin to approach graduation, these momentary payoffs become less important, and they disappear from the church. They leave because they have experienced church mostly in teenage-only appendages and have not felt connected with the congregation. They leave, in part, because they have failed to build heart connections with a broad number of significant adults.

Church as Family

Scripture refers to the body of Christ as a family (Galatians 6:10; Hebrews 2:11). Teenagers often do not feel a part of the broad church family but perhaps stand in greatest need of the warm, family-type relationships it could provide.

Scott Wilcher has a clear voice on this issue. In *The Orphaned Generation*, he says,

> The Church is not supposed to be "like a family"; it *is* a family. Rather than acting like a family, we would do well to grasp the reality that we *are* a family. ... If your congregation is going to keep its young people, the Church must see itself as a family and begin to conduct itself in that way, offering close, nurturing relationships *across generations*.[136]

Clark calls every church to "a bridging ministry intent on moving the young beyond peer experienced faith by leading them into the welcoming arms of the adoptive family of faith. The goal of even the best and most thriving youth ministry must be a strategic commitment toward authentic, inclusive and participatory adoption."[137]

---

[136]Ibid., 125.
[137]Clark, "Adoption Model of Youth Ministry."

According to Wilcher, the church needs to reflect "the heart and mind of Christ for young people—moving toward them to adopt them into the family of God, giving them a new identity as members of His family, a new purpose, a new life in a new community, no matter the cost, no matter the cultural differences, or the pain."[138] Clark adds, "To be adopted is to be fully accepted as a member of the family, with all the rights and privileges of a natural-born child."[139]

Kara Powell and her team of researchers discovered 259 churches in the U.S. doing outstanding youth ministry. Those churches share a number of characteristics. One of the most common characteristics is warmth.

> More than one research team noted that what a particular church lacks in physical resources or flashiness, it makes up in warmth, authenticity, and hospitality. ... By suggesting that churches need to grow warmer we don't mean adults should be nice to young people. Nice does not cut it. It isn't how Jesus responded to people, and it falls short of the depth we saw in congregations.
>
> Warmth is more than superficial community. It's like family. In fact, the phrase "like family" surfaced as the most common term young people used to describe their church in our interviews and field visits.[140]

Chap Clark adds:

> [T]he onus falls upon the mature in the community to initiate sustaining structures that can envelop the young person while they are within the relational cocoon of middle and high school so that they are convinced when they leave home their spiritual family,

---

[138] Wilcher, *Orphaned Generation*, 91.
[139] Clark, *Adoptive Youth Ministry*, 2.
[140] Powell, Mulder, and Griffin, *Growing Young*, 168-69.

the family of God, is always there for them, regardless of where or how they live.[141]

It is the responsibility of the mature to initiate conversations, relationships, and ministry partnership with the young.[142]

Older adults are hungry for relationships, and they want to matter in the world. Teenagers are lonely and want to be loved. Like boys and girls at a sixth-grade dance, senior adults and teenagers look across the room at each other—just a little nervous. Leaders need to gently help them start relationships. Axe mingled with Old Spice may create an aroma that will exalt Christ and bless both generations.

Relationships with adults matter, but so do relationships with children. Kara Powell's research confirmed that "the more teenagers serve and build relationships with younger children, the more likely it is that their faith will stick."[143]

Church schedules make a difference as well. Solid research says that involvement in all-church worship during high school is more consistently linked with mature faith in both high school and college than any other form of church participation.[144]

Clark summarizes the issue well: "When a faith community provides a young person with a welcoming place to belong, a meaningful way to make a difference in their world, and a family that loves and pursues them unconditionally, God's people are responding, in the name of Jesus, to the deepest core needs that a youth can experience."[145]

Transitions

A youth pastor might consider:

---

[141] Clark, "Adoption Model of Youth Ministry."
[142] Clark, *Adoptive Youth Ministry*, 245.
[143] Powell, Griffin, and Crawford, *Sticky Faith*, 75.
[144] Ibid.
[145] Clark, *Adoptive Youth Ministry*, 43.

- When I watch the eyes of adults and teenagers as they pass in the halls, what do I see? Beyond not speaking to each other, do the two generations seem almost invisible to each other?
- When we have our greeting time during Sunday morning worship, do I see teenagers and our older adults sharing hugs and greeting each other? Or do they also seem invisible to each other?

Change will not come easy. Mark Cannister has done some of the most extensive observation, study, and writing concerning movement toward intergenerational church life. The following statements are seminal:

> For a church to become intergenerational, the whole staff and the whole community, not just the student ministry, must own the initiative. This movement requires more than simply the addition of multigenerational activities. It requires a philosophical shift in the congregation's understanding of ecclesiology. Establishing intergenerational ministry as a core value necessitates a fresh discussion of the church's vision, values, and purpose.[146]
>
> Those who have made the transition from an age-specific mindset to an intergenerational mind-set agree that such a transition requires the uncompromising commitment of the church leadership. Senior pastors, associate pastors, elders, deacons, small group leaders, Sunday school teachers, and other key leaders must all be dedicated to the vision from the start. They must champion the value of becoming intergenerational until it becomes an irreplaceable mark of the congregation's identity.[147]

---

[146]Cannister, *Teenagers Matter*, 139.
[147]Ibid., 140.

Even before moving toward intergenerational programming, the senior pastor and the youth pastor can work toward changing attitudes across the congregation. For example, the pastors can lead teenagers to perform ministries that bless the congregation. Serving tables at a senior adult banquet, providing free childcare during the Christmas shopping season, and painting murals in the children's area are worthy ministries that also change perceptions of teenagers.

The way the congregation feels about the youth pastor also will help determine how they feel about teenagers. The senior adult who reports, "That youth pastor walks by me every Sunday without speaking" will have a different attitude toward the youth group than the one who says, "I couldn't believe the youth pastor came by our noon luncheon and even played a round of dominoes."

At the same time, the pastors must lead the teenagers toward an attitude adjustment. Teenagers have to change their views of adults, especially the eldest ones.

Over time, the pastors can use what they say in the pulpit or church publications to create a more positive attitude toward teenagers. They can tell brief stories of what Christ is doing in the hearts of the young. They can repeat positive things teenagers have said about their church. They can report things teenagers have done to extend the ministry of the church.

Cannister reports, "Changes are often best accomplished incrementally, as changing everything at once can be too much of a shock to the community. Casting vision, educating the congregation, and implementing small changes that the community will embrace provide an on-ramp for culture creation."[148]

Churches have spent the last fifty years increasingly designing buildings and programs to segregate age groups from one another. Perhaps the time has come for fresh thinking about ways to create rich webs of relationships around every child, teenager, and adult. One result might be 18-year-olds who love Christ's church for a lifetime and who consider the full congregation to be family.

---

[148] Ibid., 143.

Chapter 10

Congregations and the Five Functions of the Church

By Richard Ross and Jihun Han

They were continually devoting themselves to the apostles' teaching and to fellowship, to the breaking of bread and to prayer. ... And the Lord was adding to their number day by day those who were being saved.
—Acts 2:42, 47b

Youth pastors are called by God to lead the church toward worship, evangelism, discipleship, ministry, and community. A third of the time they best accomplish these five church functions as they lead teenagers into relationships and ministry with the full congregation.

Worship

Dave Wright observes, "The segregation of generations in worship is not seen in Scripture. This is a more recent development in the church. Scripture shows us examples of the people of God gathered for various acts of worship at which all ages are present."[149]

Scripture Passages

"All Israel with their elders and officers and their judges were standing on both sides of the ark. ... Then

---

[149] Dave Wright, "Gathering God's People," *Gospel-Centered Youth Ministry*, Cameron Cole and Jon Nielson, eds. (Wheaton, IL: Crossway Publishers, 2016), 103.

afterward [Joshua] read all the words of the law, the blessing and the curse, according to all that is written in the book of the law. There was not a word of all that Moses had commanded which Joshua did not read before all the assembly of Israel with the women and *the little ones* and the strangers who were living among them" (Joshua 8:33-35, emphasis added).

"Now while Ezra was praying and making confession, weeping and prostrating himself before the house of God, a very large assembly, men, women *and children*, gathered to him from Israel; for the people wept bitterly" (Ezra 10:1, emphasis added).

"And *all the people* gathered as one man at the square which was in front of the Water Gate, and they asked Ezra the scribe to bring the book of the law of Moses which the Lord had given to Israel. Then Ezra the priest brought the law before the assembly of men, women and *all who could listen with understanding....*" (Nehemiah 8:1-2, emphasis added).

"Blow a trumpet in Zion, consecrate a fast, proclaim a solemn assembly, gather the people, sanctify the congregation, assemble the elders, gather *the children* and the nursing infants. Let the bridegroom come out of his room and the bride out of her bridal chamber" (Joel 2:15-16, emphasis added).

"On the first day of the week, when we were gathered together to break bread, Paul began talking to them ... And there was *a young man* named Eutychus...." (Acts 20:7-9, emphasis added).

Rob Rienow also reports that, "When the early Christians in the New Testament era met together for their weekly worship service, they gathered with all ages together."[150]

Today

Steve Parr and Tom Crites studied both young adults who stayed in the church and those who walked away from the church. They report that, "Young adults who attended worship services that separated them from their parents when they were children were 38% more likely to have strayed as a young adult than those who were not in separate services."[151]

As noted in chapter 9, Kara Powell and her team made a similar observation: "We discovered in our previous research that involvement in all-church worship during high school is more consistently linked with mature faith in both high school and college than any other form of church participation."[152]

Chap Clark is not surprised by these observations:

> Youth ministries that establish separate youth worship services at times when the "big people" are in "big people church" are nurturing kids into a needs-based understanding of worship and the Christian faith. Not only that, but they are dividing up the body of Christ. Children, teenagers, young adults, parents, middle-aged adults, senior citizens ... all of them need to be worshiping together to experience the full breadth and depth of the body of Christ and to exercise and benefit from the giftedness of all.[153]

Rob Rienow agrees:

---

[150]Rienow, *Five Reasons*, 53.
[151]Parr and Crites, *Why They Stay*, 88.
[152]Powell, Mulder, and Griffin, *Growing Young*, 174.
[153]Clark, *Adoptive Youth Ministry*, 160.

The church service is not an adult education hour. It is a gathering of the entire multi-generational community of faith coming into the presence of God. It is a time for all ages to worship Him and to be "spiritually fed" through the worship, prayer, Scripture readings, and preaching.[154]

Kara Powell and her team discovered many churches who conducted worship services this way. One is First Baptist Church of South Gate in Los Angeles.[155] Reflecting their neighborhood, members represent a mix of first-generation Spanish-speaking immigrants from more than ten Latin American countries. The church decided to prioritize young people, even though that would mean sacrifices for the adults. Powell reports:

> What's more, young people are actively welcomed into planning for worship and special events. When it comes to special services, such as Easter, the first question is usually, "What will the young people do?" They serve in all areas of the church, from children's ministry to the weekly food pantry outreach, alongside adults. One 15-year-old girl noted, "If you want to help, they help you help."[156]

Youth pastors might consider these questions:

1. Are teenagers periodically present on platform during Sunday morning worship (praying, singing, making announcements, etc.)?
2. Do the teenagers ever add creative elements to worship (drama, interpretive movement, etc.)?

---

[154]Rienow, *Five Reasons*, 55.
[155]Powell, Mulder, and Griffin, *Growing Young*, 197-99.
[156]Ibid., 199.

3. Are teenagers visible in other ways during Sunday morning worship (ushering, greeting, etc.)?
4. Do I tell the senior pastor about subjects that are very much on the minds of our teenagers so those subjects can be worked into sermons (death of a teenager in the community, a team winning a state championship, etc.)?
5. In our greeting time during worship, do we ever encourage members to intentionally give greetings across the generations?
6. Does the senior pastor dedicate and pray over teenagers near their thirteenth birthday, in the spirit of a Bar Mitzvah?
7. Have we considered making the first Sunday of every month a First Family Sunday, with families sitting together and with all children and teenagers taking friends who attend alone to sit with those families?
8. Do we give our teenagers biblical reasons to embrace and value corporate worship that brings together all the generations?

Mark Howard summarizes the issue when he says, "Our aim is to cultivate maturing disciples of Jesus who are committed to the family of God, not simply good youth group participants. This means that as youth pastors, we need to be intentional about equipping the youth to more fully participate in and appreciate corporate worship."[157]

Discipleship

In Titus 2:1-6, Paul clearly calls the adults of the church to shape the younger generation. Even though some adults may desire

---

[157] Mark Howard, "Community Based on the Gospel," *Gospel-Centered Youth Ministry*, Cameron Cole and Jon Nielson, eds. (Wheaton, IL: Crossway Publishers, 2016), 87.

to see impact in the lives of teenagers, they may sense they have not been called to formally disciple this age group or to serve as a typical youth ministry leader. At the same time, they may gladly accept a call to invest in the life of one special teenager.

Prayer Partners

Those adults might express this call by becoming a Prayer Partner. Prayer Partners pray daily over a teenager and provide encouragement and warmth to that young person. They reflect the heart of an older Paul toward Timothy—"I constantly remember you in my prayers night and day, longing to see you ... so that I may be filled with joy" (2 Timothy 1:3-4).

The efficacy of prayer always will be the center of a Prayer Partner strategy. But prayer tends to bond hearts and can lead to a rich, life-altering relationship between a teenager and the adult who prays for him or her. Prayer Partners may move from concerted prayer to face-to-face relationships when they have the consent of parents, interest from the teenager, compliance with church policies, and the completion of Prayer Partner training.

Prayer Partners tend to say, "You can't pray every day for young people without falling in love with them." Teenagers in those relationships tend to say, "I can't believe someone not in my family loves me enough to pray for me every day."

Prayer Partners always are good for a hug after a hard week. And birthday cards show up. And teenagers get mail while on a mission trip.

Later, a teenager gets out of school to go to the Prayer Partner's funeral and sits up front with the family. And it's the whole church just being the church.

This strategy goes far beyond just connecting one teenager with one member of the congregation. This strategy can lead to immersing the youth group into the full congregation. The following background can make this statement believable.

Teenagers tend to form groups of close friends with approximately four to eight members. Teenagers often view their group, or cluster, as essential to their survival.

Here is an important fact. Teenagers will accept any adult as trustworthy if a member of their cluster says he or she can be trusted. Therefore, when a teenager at church forms a heart connection with a Prayer Partner, then that adult slowly can become valuable to all the members of the teenager's cluster.

At the same time, all of the other members of the cluster are growing in relationship with their Prayer Partners and introducing their partners to the cluster. Thus, the number of linkages between the generations can increase exponentially over time.

Prayer Partners and the Future

Use your imagination.

- Imagine a pipeline of Christ's power and protection flowing into your teenagers' lives every day through prayer.
- Imagine more adults praying the second year than the first, and more the third year than the second.
- Imagine your teenagers receiving regular notes of encouragement from the very people who care enough to pray for them every day.
- Imagine teenagers who are stronger and steadier in their faith because they feel the prayers and support of their Prayer Partners.
- Imagine having a Prayer Partner you quickly can email anytime you learn of a crisis affecting that Partner's teenager.
- Imagine having a host of Prayer Partners you quickly can email anytime there is a great challenge or opportunity facing the overall youth ministry.
- Imagine knowing adults are praying for a young generation to lead the church in an awakening to God's Son.

Many teenagers today are missing relationships that could be valuable to them. Prayer Partners can be part of the solution. They can:

- Introduce their teenager to their extended family.
- Introduce their teenager to other members of the congregation who can bless his or her life.
- Introduce their teenager to adults who can help open doors related to education, present employment, and future vocation.

Relationships are powerful, but prayer is the heart of Prayer Partner relationships. Those prayers can flow in both directions. Teenagers who develop heart connections with their Partner may well begin to pray for him or her. Adults can discover there is power in prayer as a teenager brings the Partner's name before the Throne every morning. Over time, that may well mean prayer requests begin to flow both directions.

A Prayer Partner initiative is built on four commitments:

1. For an adult Prayer Partner to pray for his assigned teenager every day.
2. For the adult Prayer Partner to continue to pray for his assigned teenager until he graduates from high school or college or is married.
3. For the Prayer Partner to encourage his teenager with spoken words and notes that communicate, "I'm still here and I'm still praying for you."
4. For teenagers to reciprocate those actions toward their adult.

Keys to Effectiveness

Churches that have embraced a Prayer Partner initiative have discovered:

1. The senior pastor's excitement about and commitment to the initiative are most important to a successful ministry.
2. The youth pastor's passionate concern for having every teenager covered in daily prayer is the second most important ingredient.
3. A gifted, motivated Prayer Partner initiative coordinator is the third most important factor. With the support of the church staff, the coordinator works through leaders in adult ministry and youth ministry, arranges for background checks, forms the same-gender pairs, and creates plans for introducing the two generations to each other.
4. A well-crafted communication/promotion plan is the fourth most important key.

Evangelism and Ministry

Discipleship should always lead to service and ministry. The Dead Sea is dead because it has no outlet; water runs in but does not run out. Every discipleship initiative ultimately should point toward action.

Mobilizing Teenagers

Church leaders often tell children (who are wet cement), "Sit still and listen and then you can serve someday." Then leaders tell teenagers (who are wet cement), "Continue to sit still and listen and then you can serve someday." Then the cement hardens. Finally, leaders say to adults: "Get up and serve." But the challenge is pointless. Those who sit passively for eighteen years are likely to do so for the rest of their lives.

Equipping and releasing teenagers to lead is so valuable that every teenager needs that experience. Every teenager. Burns and DeVries believe: "Ministry and leadership are not just for the all-stars. Our calling is to help every student have an opportunity in which he or she can serve and experience the joy of ministry."[158] Clark adds that "all kids have gifts, talents, vision, and energy to bring to the family table."[159]

If the church only plans to train the all-stars to be leaders, the youth pastor can probably handle that alone. But if the mission is to equip every teenager to fulfill his calling, many more parents and other adults need to be involved. Dave Rahn calls for "every [teenage] leader to have the benefit of an adult partner/mentor/friend to walk with in this ministry. This is the best of all worlds—mature adult leadership encouraging, equipping, and ultimately validating [teenage] leadership."[160]

Church leaders like to say, "Teenagers are not the church of tomorrow. They are the church today." But those words usually are not tied to action. Few teenagers are invited to use their gifts and abilities to bless and impact the full church. While addressing the 2014 National Youth Workers Convention, Mark Matlock said, "Youth ministry reminds the church that teens are not marginalized members of the body but are co-creators and conspirators in the divine work of the church, restoring life on earth as it is in heaven."

But too often the church misses what the service of teenagers could have meant to the Kingdom. Cannister says, "I fear that we have forgotten what the splendor of church looks and feels like because we have segregated age groups for so long. We have accepted a new definition of normal, in which children and teenagers are spectators in most settings and contributors only in their age-appropriate contexts."[161]

Many churches underestimate the potential of teenagers. Noted researcher Robert Epstein reports, "We know from extensive research both in the U.S. and elsewhere that when we treat teens

---

[158]Jim Burns and Mike DeVries, *The Youth Builder* (Ventura, CA: Gospel Light Publications, 2002), 144.
[159]Clark, *Adoptive Youth Ministry*, 8.
[160]Kenda Dean, Chap Clark, and Dave Rahn, eds. *Starting Right: Thinking Theologically about Youth Ministry* (Grand Rapids, MI: 2001), 175.
[161]Cannister, *Teenagers Matter*, 123.

like adults, they almost immediately rise to the challenge."[162] Teenagers absolutely can be trained to lead. They just need an adult who will use a process similar to this:

1. I do it, and you watch.
2. I do it, and you assist.
3. You do it, and I assist.
4. You do it, and I do something else.

Lifetime Faith

Teenagers who serve with the congregation are more likely to develop a lifetime faith. Parr and Crites report from their study of young adults, "When asked why they have stayed in church, the second most common self-described reason for staying was that they are 'personally serving' in a leadership position at their church."[163]

The Barna organization reports:

> Effective ministry to Millennials means helping these young believers discover their own mission in the world, not merely asking them to wait their turn.... Millennials who remain active in church are twice as likely as dropouts to say they served the poor through their church (33% versus 14%). They are also ... more likely to indicate they had found a cause or issue at church that motivates them (24% versus 10%).[164]

Kara Powell's "Sticky Faith" study led her to report, "... The survey shows that if teenagers served in middle school or children's

---

[162] Robert Epstein, "The Myth of the Teen Brain," June 1, 2007, scientificamerican.com.
[163] Parr and Crites, *Why They Stay*, 116.
[164] Barna Group, "5 Ways to Connect with Millennials," September 9, 2014, barna.org.

ministry while they were in high school, their faith seemed to be 'stickier' in college."[165] Powell's later "growing young" study revealed:

> When interview participants in our study were asked what makes their church effective with young people, nearly 60 percent named service practices, missional practices, or generally being outward oriented. Further, when we asked leaders, "What is a practice in your congregation that indicates commitment from or growth in young people?" nearly 70 percent named young people serving in some way.[166]

Having leadership roles accelerates a teenager's growth toward a lasting faith. This fact can motivate leaders to gently open more leadership roles for teenagers at church. Dave Rahn points out:

> The Bible teaches that every believer has been given gifts to be used on behalf of the church (Romans 14; 1 Corinthians 12-14; Ephesians 4). The Bible does not teach that such gifts and resulting service are hidden like time-release capsules in the lives of Christians—inoperable until they reach the age of 20 (or 40!). At the very least this suggests that we must begin early (in youth ministry), to help identify, nurture, foster, and utilize the gifts God has given the young in the church.[167]

Veteran youth leaders Jim Burns and Mike DeVries add,

> Students need to see that they're not the church of tomorrow; rather, their gifts, abilities and services are needed today. We must do everything we can to

---

[165] Powell, Griffin, and Crawford, *Sticky Faith*, 75.
[166] Powell, Mulder, and Griffin, *Growing Young*, 242.
[167] Dean, Clark, and Rahn, *Starting Right*, 173.

assimilate students into the life of the church. Looking back, youth ministry in the past has been far too isolated from the big church.[168]

Ministry and Evangelism Possibilities

Possible leadership roles vary by church, but they may include such things as:

- Teenagers taking public roles in worship leadership.
- Teenagers actively participating in meetings where church business is conducted.
- Teenagers serving on boards and committees.
- Teenagers serving on church evangelism teams.
- Teenagers serving on church servant ministry teams.
- Teenagers going on church mission trips.
- Teenagers leading Bible classes for children.
- Teenagers tutoring children at risk for academic failure.
- Teenagers ministering with special-needs children or adults.

Most churches could do much better in creating entirely new environments where the spiritual transformation of teenagers could take place. Chap Clark provides a specific illustration:

> When a small group leader, for example, discovers that a high school junior is a gifted audio technician, then that leader may use that knowledge to find a way to connect that junior to the group of people who are responsible for the worship sound production. The key to this strategy, however, is not to simply use a young person's skill or interest to connect them to a task, but rather the tech team is tasked with adopting the teen as a member of the family of God. The junior thinks

---

[168]Burns and DeVries, *The Youth Builder*, 138.

that they are there just to help run the audio mix, but the other adults realize, and are even trained in this, to be literal adopters of that teenager. Spiritual practices (prayer, sharing, even a Bible study) then become a routine part of their work and everyone welcomes the young person as if they were their little brother or sister, or "adopted" child.[169]

Key Questions

Wise youth pastors consider questions such as these:

1. Do I believe the Holy Spirit indwells all believers, including children and teenagers, at the time of their conversion?

2. Do I believe the Holy Spirit instills spiritual gifts in all believers, including children and teenagers, at the time of their conversion?

3. Do I believe God calls all believers, including children and teenagers, to join Him in bringing in His Kingdom at the time of their conversion?

4. Do I believe I have a biblical mandate to call out and equip every teenager to join Christ in Kingdom service *today*, using his or her spiritual gifts?

5. Do I believe every teenager in our ministry should be able to articulate his spiritual gifts and calling in ministry?

6. Have I led the church toward recognizing a teenager's thirteenth birthday as a Bar Mitzvah-type

---

[169]Clark, "The Adoption Model."

moment so that adults will welcome teenagers as *young adult* partners in ministry?

7. Do I continually interact with the leaders of children's and adult ministries in order to open doors for teenagers to serve?

8. Do I have in my office a way of tracking which teenagers are serving in the broader church and which are not?

9. When I plan toward evangelism strategies, do I consider whether our purpose is best served by age-specific or intergenerational plans?

10. When I plan toward servant ministry strategies, do I consider whether our purpose is best served by age-specific or intergenerational plans?

11. When I plan toward mission trips in the U.S. or globally, do I consider whether our purpose is best served by age-specific or intergenerational plans?

12. Do I plan with those in children's ministry to ensure that there is unbroken training related to spiritual gifts—and an unbroken focus on Kingdom service in the broader church—as children become teenagers?

13. Because our teenagers experience the joy and challenge of service in the broader church, are they now motivated to receive even more discipling and leadership training?

14. Because our teenagers can articulate their specific callings, embrace their spiritual gifts, perform

valuable Kingdom service, connect to the full congregation, and appear valuable by God's people—do I sense they will adore Christ, love the church, and make a Kingdom impact all their lives?

Community

All of chapter 9 focused on the church function of "community." To all that was said there, Chap Clark adds this word:

> If [teenagers] are a part of the church today—which means siblings with other members—they need opportunities and environments to participate, explore, and experience relationships within the entire church. They need exposure to spaces outside the walls of the youth room. They need to interact with those who have earned their gray hairs, make decisions alongside middle-aged folks, and, of course, join in the changing of babies' diapers.[170]

Conclusion

Veteran youth ministry professor Wes Black sees the big picture when he says,

> Youth ministry is a church-wide ministry that involves teenagers in all the functions of the church. These functions include worship, evangelism, fellowship, discipleship, ministry, and missions. Taken together, these provide a comprehensive picture of the Christian life. As youths participate in church-wide events, they experience the purposes and functions on a larger scale. They see the scope of the Christian life through

---

[170] Clark, *Adoptive Youth Ministry*, 338.

many ages. They build images and memories of role models for many aspects of life.[171]

A teenage Jaquelle Crowe would shout "Amen!" She says:

> It's almost like teenaged Jesus-followers are led to believe that we're not really part of the church; we're just served by it. But if our whole purpose of going to church is to get our needs met, we have a big problem. The truth is, if we're part of the body, we have a responsibility to the entire body. If teenagers love Jesus, we should be committed to his whole church.[172]

Mike McGarry provides a fitting summary when he declares, "... A church must not see ministry to teens as something delegated to the 'youth leaders.' Instead, the whole church should place a high value on intentionally welcoming the coming generations and encouraging them to meaningfully contribute to the life of the church."[173]

---

[171] Wes Black, "The Preparatory Approach to Youth Ministry," *Four Views of Youth Ministry and the Church*, Mark Senter, ed. (Grand Rapids, MI: Zondervan, 2001), 55.
[172] Crowe, *This Changes Everything*, 48-49.
[173] Mike McGarry, "Building a Foundation with the Parents," *Gospel-Centered Youth Ministry*, Cameron Cole and Jon Nielson, eds. (Wheaton, IL: Crossway Publishers, 2016), 95.

Chapter 11

Intergenerational Programming

By Richard Ross

And even when I am old and gray, O God, do not forsake me, until I declare your strength to this generation, your power to all who are to come.
—Psalm 71:18

According to Allen and Ross, "Intergenerational ministry occurs when a congregation intentionally brings the generations together in mutual serving, sharing, or learning within the core activities of the church in order to live out being the body of Christ to each other and the greater community."[174]

A vision for shifting some church programming in an intergenerational direction must begin with the senior pastor. He likely will be the first to ask, "Are we prepared to establish intergenerational community as a core value? On what specific occasions will we bring the various generations together? How will we help them know each other across generational lines? Once they are together and relationships have begun, how will we guide them to experience life in the body of Christ together?"

Balancing Ministry

Teenagers need certain times when they are applying the principles of Scripture to life in a high school, to bodies that are sexually developing, to relationships with peers, to their approaching vocational choices, to their preparation for marriage or singlehood,

---

[174]Holly Catterton Allen and Christine Lawton Ross, *Intergenerational Christian Formation* (Downers Grove, IL: InterVarsity Press, 2012), 17.

and so on. Teenagers need environments that allow them to be shaped by godly peers who are role models. Teenagers need to create evangelistic outreaches that are relevant to lost teenagers.

As with all other areas of church life, strategic thinking is the key. Pastors and other church leaders continually must consider this question: "Will the specific ministry impact we desire in this particular case be best achieved through an age-specific program or an intergenerational one?"

Guiding Change

Leading a church to change is somewhat like turning an aircraft carrier. Sharp turns are not practical. Trying to force God's people to make immediate changes causes conflict, damages the church, and does not help teenagers. Youth pastors, parents, and leaders need to develop a prayer-saturated, long-term plan for gently leading a church toward more intergenerational programming.

As noted earlier, the senior pastor is pivotal to any change in an intergenerational direction. For one thing, one age-group pastor might clearly see the Kingdom advantages of moving in such directions, and another age-group pastor might not. As peers, age-group pastors may have a difficult time developing a unified direction. It may fall to the senior pastor to teach, lead, and mentor until all the pastors have embraced a vision for bringing the generations together.

In addition, the senior pastor must ensure the youth pastor (and other age-group pastors) is not placed at risk with the congregation as a result of this seismic shift. At present:

- Teenagers have been culturalized to believe that being only with peers is "more fun" than being with all generations. Therefore, they may affirm a youth pastor who will give them what they presently want.

Intergenerational Programming

- Teenagers who are happy with age-segregated events tend to say positive things about the youth pastor at home. This leads to parents' affirming the youth pastor.
- Members of the congregation who only have an older view of youth ministry love hearing about the "wonderful activities for our youth." This may lead them to affirm (and give raises to) the youth pastor who keeps groups segregated.

The senior pastor must lead the stakeholders of the church to grasp a new perspective on youth ministry. Otherwise, the youth pastor who is moving in more intergenerational directions may wake up to an unpleasant life. He may discover that instead of pats on the head he now is getting criticism. He may learn that members of the congregation are beginning to say he is not doing what he was called to do. Worst case, he may learn that some even are discussing his termination.

Temporarily, a totally age-segregated approach to youth ministry looks cooler, more exciting, and more appealing to teenagers. At times, it may result in better attendance. All this makes the youth pastor a hero. But the research is clear. On average, teenagers who spend six years mostly with other teenagers do not stay connected to the church or walk in faith the rest of their lives.

The senior pastor must lead the congregation through a careful study of Scripture on the true nature of the church. And he must ask questions as specific as:

- Would we rather see one hundred teenagers active today, knowing the majority will fall away from the church and not walk in faith in adulthood; or would we rather see eighty active today, knowing that most of them will live as true disciples all their lives?
- Are we going to give our affirmations and financial support to age-group pastors who make a temporary splash or to our pastors who lead us to build lifetime disciples?

The church has been divided into age-group compartments for decades. Small steps in the direction of intergenerational church life work better than major changes. As noted in chapter 9, changing everything at once can be a shock to a church, while small changes can keep everyone positive about the future.[175]

For specific help in moving to a more intergenerational ministry, see:

- Allen, Holly Catterton and Christine Lawton Ross. *Intergenerational Christian Formation*. Downers Grove, IL: InterVarsity Press, 2012.
- Cannister, Mark. *Teenagers Matter: Making Student Ministry a Priority in the Church*. Grand Rapids, MI: Baker Academic, 2013.
- Clark, Chap, ed. *Youth Ministry in the 21st Century: Five Views*. Grand Rapids, MI: Baker Academic, 2015.
- Wilcher, Scott. *The Orphaned Generation: The Father's Heart for Connecting Youth and Young Adults to Your Church*. Chesapeake, VA: UpStream Project, 2010.

Conclusion

Even when change is slow and measured, the senior pastor and the youth pastor know where they are moving. Their prayer may be:

"As the day of Christ's return draws near,
let us not be found in faith communities divided by age,
but let us unwaveringly take hold of the fact that in Christ Jesus:
We are the family of God
and he has called us together to be one in him
that we might be formed into the likeness of his Son,
enabled to worship him in unity
and be the light of Christ in this dark world."[176]

---

[175] Cannister, *Teenagers Matter*, 143.
[176] Allen and Ross, *Intergenerational Christian Formation*, 272.

PART 3

Ministry with Teenagers as a Youth Group

Chapter 12

Evangelism, Ministry, and Missions

By Richard Ross and Oluwaseun A. Oladipupo

You shall be My witnesses both in Jerusalem, and in all Judea and Samaria, and even to the remotest part of the earth.
—Acts 1:8b

Greg Stier has one of the clearest voices in the nation related to evangelizing teenagers. His core message to youth pastors is this:

> God has given you a mission, your specific piece of advancing THE Cause of Christ in your own community. You must identify it, relentlessly pray over it and do everything you can in the power of Christ to accomplish it. There is a generation of teenagers in your midst who are literally on the highway to hell, and you and I have the message that can rescue them from it! Don't lose sight of this vital mission that God has placed firmly in your made-worthy-by-the-blood-of-Christ hands![177]

The widely accepted Lausanne Covenant defines evangelism this way: "To evangelize is to spread the good news that Jesus Christ died for our sins and was raised from the dead according to the scriptures, and that as the reigning Lord he now offers the

---

[177] Greg Stier, *Gospelize Your Youth Ministry* (Arvada, CO: Dare 2 Share, 2015), 252.

forgiveness of sins and the liberating gift of the spirit to all who repent and believe."[178]

Ministries may drift in lots of other directions, but they will not drift toward a priority on evangelism. Introducing teenagers and others to Christ will become a core value only because youth pastors have provided genuine, dramatic leadership in that direction.

Evangelism Begins with the Youth Pastor

Youth pastors may need to forget the word *send*. Youth pastors cannot send teenagers and leaders to share their faith; they can only lead them. Youth pastors must follow in the footsteps of Paul, who said, "Be imitators of me, just as I also am of Christ" (1 Corinthians 11:1). Stier points out that:

> The disciples were bold in proclaiming the truth, because Jesus modeled boldness in proclaiming the truth. The same is true of you with your teenagers. If your teenagers are not engaged in prayer and relational evangelism, you need a mirror, not a bullhorn, because it starts with you, not them.[179]

Ben Trueblood says it this way:

> Your ministry is on the road to health when your students begin to think more evangelistically. This is something that is caught and taught, but too often our ministries just focus on the "taught" side of things. Students need to see healthy evangelism modeled as well. They will focus on what they see you doing far more than what they hear you saying.[180]

---

[178]Quoted in Mark Dever, *Nine Marks*, 135.
[179]Stier, *Gospelize Your Youth Ministry*, 61.
[180]Ben Trueblood, *Student Ministry That Matters: Three Elements of a Healthy Student Ministry* (Nashville, TN: LifeWay, 2016), 26.

Permit me to speak directly: If you do not share your faith on your own time, and if you do not take teenagers out to evangelize, this is a *crisis*. Put everything on hold and aggressively find someone to train you and take you out to share your faith. All your future ministry hinges on it. You *never* will create an evangelistic youth ministry if this discipline is not in your life. You never will fool others. Just confess the deficit and get trained. Now.

Then, and only then, you can ask:

1. Do our youth ministry leaders tend to share their faith on their own time and as a part of youth gatherings and outreaches? If not, then how can I give them opportunities to observe my modeling?
2. Do our teenagers tend to share their faith on their own time and as a part of youth gatherings and outreaches? If not, how can we give them opportunities to observe the modeling of their disciplers and leaders, including me?

Evangelism as a Priority

Jesus said, "For the Son of Man has come to seek and to save that which was lost" (Luke 19:10). That was the heart of Jesus and His goal. But Greg Stier notes, "The modern youth ministry model has largely abandoned the focus of Jesus and delivers, instead, a series of competing programs. We have exchanged mission for meetings. We have separated evangelism and discipleship. We have turned outreach into a program, instead of a lifestyle."[181]

In one large study, only 20 percent of youth pastors named evangelism as a high priority.[182] In another study, only 24 percent

---

[181] Greg Stier, "A Gospel-Advancing Ministry Model," *Youth Ministry in the 21st Century: Five Views*, ed. Chap Clark (Grand Rapids, MI: Baker Academic, 2015), Kindle version.
[182] George Barna, "The Priorities, Challenges, and Trends in Youth Ministry," April 6, 2016, barna.org.

did.[183] Consequently, youth ministry professor Alvin Reid reports that evangelism rates among teenagers have been steadily dropping since the 1970s.[184]

Doug Fields notes that "youth ministries that are successful in reaching unchurched students view evangelism as essential and not as just a good idea."[185] Rahn and Linhart add, "If evangelism is seen as one more thing to do, it only contributes to the burdensome pile-on that so many of us experience in ministry."[186] True discipleship leads to making evangelism a priority. And evangelism leads to an even greater desire for discipleship.

Some youth ministries consistently introduce teenagers to Jesus, and some youth ministries do so rarely. Researchers Dave Rahn and Terry Linhart wanted to understand what made those ministries different. After careful research, they discovered that youth groups can be divided into four groups.

1. The Love Flowing Stage—Teenagers love one another but typically do not reach out.
2. The Peer Encouragement Stage—Teenagers help one another with problems but seldom reach out.
3. The God-at-Work Stage—Teenagers expect to see God moving in their lives and in the lives of others. Their attention turns outward.
4. The Evangelism Expectancy Stage—Teenagers expect to see God move through them consistently to bring new ones to Christ. Teenagers pray almost daily for opportunities to share their faith.[187]

---

[183] George Barna, *The State of Youth Ministry* (Ventura, CA: The Barna Group, 2016), 12.
[184] Reid, *Raising the Bar*, 38.
[185] Doug Fields, *Purpose-Driven Youth Ministry: 9 Essential Foundations for Healthy Growth* (Grand Rapids, MI: Zondervan, 1998), 103.
[186] Rahn and Linhart, *Evangelism Remixed*, 15.
[187] Ibid., 137–41.

Once leaders sense which stage their youth group would fall in, the time comes to think carefully about moving to the next level.

Evangelistic Youth Ministries

Genuinely evangelistic youth ministries share several characteristics. Those characteristics include prayer, Scripture, Gospel stories, teenagers who bring friends, and relying on God.

Prayer
Rahn and Linhart report that:

> The key practice that distinguishes evangelistically fruitful student leaders from others is their patterns of prayer. Examine the lives of student leaders who are effectively reaching others for Christ and you'll find young people who are praying. At the moment a student begins to interact with God for the sake of seeing another come to Christ, a change takes place.[188]

"These all with one mind were continually devoting themselves to prayer..." (Acts 1:14). Prayer was the key as the early church reached scores of lost people every day. Something similar can happen in ministry with a lost generation today. When teenage believers gather, they should pray specifically for the lost.

> When we pray and teach our students to pray, we are connecting them with the One who can transform not only their lives, but the lives of their friends, classmates, teammates, family members and coworkers. When prayer becomes the engine, and not the caboose of our youth ministry efforts, then we'll start getting

---
[188]Ibid., 90.

serious traction toward building Gospel Advancing Ministries.[189]

Scripture

One research study revealed that Bible-soaked youth groups tend to see many teenagers come to Jesus. The researchers reported, "A key distinctive of these groups was the centrality of the Bible. They were committed to providing clear, biblical teaching each week. ... The teens saw Scripture as a guiding force, one of the main methods of discovering what God expected of them."[190]

Closely related, the teenagers who had led more than four friends to Christ regularly memorized Scripture. The implications are that these teenagers were not only equipped with tools. They also practiced learning Scripture to use with their friends as they shared.[191]

Gospel Stories

Youth ministries become more evangelistic when teenagers often hear stories about the propagation of the Gospel. Stier provides this challenge to youth pastors, parents, and leaders:

> We need more stories in youth group, small groups and Sunday school—real life stories, from real life teenagers, sharing the real life gospel conversations they're having with their peers! ... This is a time where teenagers can share stories—good, bad or ugly—about someone they are praying for, pursuing and/or persuading with Jesus' message of grace.[192]

---

[189]Stier, *Gospelize Your Youth Ministry*, 59.
[190]Rahn and Linhart, *Evangelism Remixed*, 125.
[191]Ibid., 126.
[192]Stier, *Gospelize Your Youth Ministry*, 221.

Teenage Believers Who Bring Friends

Teenagers need to know they can bring friends to worship and to youth ministry events to hear how to meet Jesus. The research says teenagers who lead the most people to Christ invite lost friends to come almost weekly. They know meetings will have quality, and they know the Gospel will be presented.

They also know they can introduce their friends to individual youth leaders for more conversations about Christ. Therefore, making adult leaders available for communicating the Gospel is crucial to developing evangelistically effective teenagers.

Relying on God

Sharing Christ with friends forces teenage disciples to rely on God. Stier notes why this is vital:

> If you give the average teenager a choice to go to the Amazon to build a mud hut for the poor while fighting off hungry Pythons, or going to their school cafeteria and dropping the "J Bomb" on a group of their friends, most teenagers would pick the pythons. Why? Because the average teenager would rather risk getting choked by a giant snake, than getting choked out of their social circle![193]

Training to Share the Gospel

Teenagers need to know what to say to friends who do not know Christ. Rahn and Linhart say, "Verbal witnessing is the central method God has chosen to spread the good news of Jesus Christ (2 Cor. 5:11–21). … Effective evangelistic youth groups carry out regular training efforts—be they formal or informal in nature—to help students learn how to become a verbal witness."[194]

Greg Stier provides more detail:

---

[193] Stier, "A Gospel-Advancing Ministry Model," Kindle version.
[194] Rahn and Linhart, *Evangelism Remixed*, 119.

> For teenagers to develop a lifestyle of evangelism, they need to be equipped to share their faith. This includes knowing how to naturally bring up the gospel, explain it clearly, tie in their story, and navigate various responses to the gospel. They also need to learn how to ask great questions and listen deeply to others. ... Of course, this takes time, prayer, patience and coaching.[195]

Church Support for Evangelism with Teenagers

Lost Teenagers Who Act Nice

Most adults in the congregation mildly want to see teenagers come to faith in Christ. Most enjoy hearing teenagers sometimes meet Jesus on church property. They know for teenagers to be redeemed at church, they first have to arrive lost. But there may be limits to their compassion.

Few adults would announce this aloud, but some might prefer lost teenagers to arrive in very small numbers. (And they would want them to look sharp and mostly act nice.) Bottom line, they would not want to see too many pre-Christians "change things," act badly, or negatively impact the personality of the youth group. This is the polar opposite from Paul, who declared, "For I could wish that I myself were accursed, separated from Christ for the sake of my brethren, my kinsmen according to the flesh" (Romans 9:3).

Many a pastor has had angry parishioners in his office, insisting he do something about all those "outsiders" who are beginning to attend the youth group. Some of those who are upset may simply be spiritually shallow. But some, especially parents, may have valid concerns. They honestly may believe their teenage child is in danger of spiritual or emotional harm.

---

[195]Stier, "A Gospel-Advancing Ministry Model," Kindle version.

The senior pastor can take the lead on this issue. He will tend to have more influence with adults than the youth pastor. At the same time, the senior pastor has to let adults know that he and the youth pastor hear their voices and that the pastors will respond to their concerns.

The senior pastor and the youth pastor need to search for ways to fulfill the Great Commission but also to maintain a uniquely Christlike environment that is spiritually, morally, and emotionally safe. They can discuss questions such as the following:

1. When a community teenager first arrives, can we have adults prepared to meet that teenager and then to start a sincere friendship with him or her? (Of course, this would be in addition to having teenagers trained to watch for and to welcome new attendees.)
2. Do we need to increase the number of leaders and sponsors who attend youth gatherings and events, primarily to minister but also to provide gentle structure?
3. Do we need a positive but clear list of discipline guidelines for those times when teenagers are together? How can we lead our own teenagers and leaders to gently guide visitors to know how the group operates?
4. How will we lead godly families to adopt "spiritual orphans" early on, thus providing additional relationships that provide structure?
5. How can Sunday morning sermons lead the congregation to see the church as a hospital for sinners more than a country club for saints?

Cross-Cultural Ministry

Shallow church members may want to reach only "our kind of people." If a critical mass of members wants to worship with only their race, the membership may differ significantly from the immediate church community.

Consistent with the discussion above, this complicated issue calls for the engagement of the senior pastor. Church members (especially powerful ones) who embrace an unbiblical view of people are not likely to turn to the youth pastor for correction. The senior pastor, in the pulpit, preaching directly from the Word of God, offers the best probability for change.

Age-group pastors need concrete ways for the church to grant them freedom to reach diverse members of the next generation. More than a few have been completely blindsided by a termination for effectively reaching "the wrong kind of people."

Campus Evangelism

Greg Stier is right on target when he says, "...In a very real sense, your teenagers go on a mission trip every day when they walk into their schools. And, for many of them, this is a scarier trip than traveling hundreds or thousands of miles to some dangerous, foreign country."[196]

Most teenage believers are most immersed in relationships for the most number of hours while at school. Their campus thus becomes one of the most natural places for them to tell friends about Jesus. Prayer, training, and role models give them the courage they need to share. Youth pastors who have hearts for campus impact are essential. The following steps can allow them to start or strengthen such ministry:

1. The youth pastor assembles other youth leaders from the area to pray deeply.
2. All the youth leaders in the area assemble their teenage disciples to pray together.
3. The youth leaders and young disciples agree on the broad strategy they hear God giving them.

---

[196] Stier, *Gospelize Your Youth Ministry*, 48.

4. Teenage disciples from a particular school meet alongside youth leaders from churches in that community to agree on a specific strategy for that school.
5. This group determines if existing ministries in the school already are sharing the Gospel with lost teenagers. If they are, then the group plans how to mobilize teenage disciples in community churches to join those existing ministries and thus accelerate the harvest.
6. If the group determines that there are no existing ministries, or that existing ministries are simply devotional and not evangelistic, then the group sets a plan for beginning a new ministry.

Churches, organizations, and teenagers have two ways to reach out to a school. Some teenagers and leaders start outreach clubs, which are recognized as official groups and are allowed to meet on campus. Others, out of necessity, organize campus outreaches that usually meet after school or in the evenings in churches, homes, or other venues.

In either case, the focus is on teenagers reaching out to friends at the school and having one-on-one conversations about Christ. All this is championed by a network of area youth pastors who train and support the teenagers.

Missions

The local church, and thus youth ministry, exists:

1. To exalt Christ globally—the supreme purpose of missions.
2. To mobilize believers for God's mission.
3. To make disciples among all nations.
4. To reach every unreached people with the Gospel.
5. To plant churches among those peoples.

6. Ultimately, to complete God's commission to the church.

What does it look like for a teenager to have God's heart for the nations? Ben Trueblood answers this way:

1. They understand and can articulate the Gospel.
2. They understand that the Gospel is meant to reach beyond them and their immediate circle.
3. They have predetermined to say "yes" to God in whatever He calls them to do or wherever He calls them to go.
4. They begin to care less about the things of this world because their gaze is becoming more and more fixed on Jesus.
5. They begin to use the platforms God has given them in their daily lives as opportunities to share the Gospel.
6. They become less and less content with what many (unfortunately) may see as normal Christianity.
7. They will want to bring others along with them in their pursuit of taking Jesus to the ends of the earth.
8. They will want to go to the nations, and if that isn't possible, they will find a way to be connected to what God is doing around the world.[197]

The Compassion of Christ
Teenage disciples who follow Jesus will share His heart for those in need. Cole and Nielson note, "It's clear that the Bible instructs God's people to serve the poor. If we want students to practice a biblical faith, youth leaders must train and equip them to serve the poor in a way that is helpful and honors God. This is a matter, simply, of obedience to God's Word!"[198]

---
[197]Trueblood, *Student Ministry That Matters*, 127-28.
[198]Cole and Nielson, *Gospel-Centered*, 180.

Stier would agree with compassion toward the total person: "Get [your teenagers] to feed the poor with bread AND the Bread of Life. Have them pass out water for the body AND Living Water for the soul. Get your teenagers to build houses for the poor on earth AND ones in heaven too."[199]

Meeting someone's practical need only as a sneaky way to present the Gospel is not the compassion of Christ. On the other hand, only meeting practical needs and never sharing the Good News also is disobedient to Scripture. Teenage disciples sacrificially care for others. And they always direct attention to Jesus as the Spirit leads.

Short-Term Mission Trips

Researchers Rahn and Linhart report that:

> Evangelistic youth ministries consistently named short-term mission trips as the activity that contributes most to their evangelistic success. Short-term missions provide powerful opportunities to see God at work and to learn how to rely on the Holy Spirit while reaching out to others. ... It became a wake-up call for some to commit their lives to serving God and his purposes.[200]

Not all short-term trips make that kind of impact. But when leaders give prayerful attention to the content and the quality of those trips, they can have a powerful role in calling out and training young believers to share their faith—far away and near to home.

In addition, such trips build disciples. As with the apostles, discipleship for teenagers may begin with a journey (Mark 6:7). Taking teenagers on a trip that tests their faith and breaks their hearts may be the first step in turning them into disciples.

---

[199]Stier, *Gospelize Your Youth Ministry*, 182.
[200]Rahn and Linhart, *Evangelism Remixed*, 127–28.

When planning toward short-term trips, Cole and Nielson provide valuable guidance:

> Don't try to be a trailblazer; partner with a known ministry. ... Always ask first if hosting a team would be helpful to them and how you could support the ongoing work that God is already doing. This protects against a design-your-own ministry experience mentality, which is almost always rooted in pride and pragmatism, rather than a desire to form long-term partnerships that actually enhance and encourage established ministry workers.[201]

A Longer Missions Experience

Virtually every disciple should go on short-term mission projects throughout the teenage years and beyond. But at least once, every teenager should consider the life-altering challenge of going to the front lines for a longer period. A youth pastor might envision it becoming normative in his church that almost every student serve full-time in domestic or international missions for a summer, semester, or year, around age 18 or 19.

Those just out of high school know they are living a brief and unique chapter of their lives. These are the years in between the structure of high school and the coming responsibilities of a permanent job and family. These short years provide an opportunity for a longer missions experience that can accelerate growth toward adulthood, sharpen future goals, and impact Christ's Kingdom.

Longer mission trips allow teenagers to build deep relationships with people. They can experience firsthand the suffering some believers willingly accept for Christ's name. They can see how crushing poverty affects the daily lives of those they have come to love. They can learn, perhaps for the first time, what it means to join Christ in His sufferings (Philippians 3:10).

---

[201] Cole and Nielson, *Gospel-Centered*, 196.

Students returning home also may have a different perspective on life's purpose. They may choose to live as missionaries wherever life takes them. Those who have invested in a "mission field" are much more likely to view their own neighborhoods and workplaces as fields "white for harvest" (John 4:35).

Eighteen-year-olds crave a grand adventure. They are ready to do hard things and go to the hard places. This is the perfect time for an assignment so challenging it requires all they are and all the Spirit supplies.

Society increasingly is using the term *gap year* to refer to a student who takes time from university studies for an extended trip or some immersive experience. Increasingly, universities are granting admission to high school graduates but not requiring them to register for classes for one year. That period might easily become an extended missions adventure.

Stemming the Tide of Dropouts

Church attendance among high school seniors falls precipitously during the final months before graduation. Preparation for a missions adventure soon after high school could become an exciting, energizing focus for one's senior year at church.

Leaders could introduce the year by asking new seniors, "Are you fully prepared to share Christ in a clear way with any person you meet? Do you feel competent to answer many of the tough questions people may have about the Bible? Are you so consistent in your morning worship and Bible study that your quiet time sustains you during lonely or difficult days?" Seniors recognizing they need much training before going out to a challenging assignment may remain active through graduation and beyond.

Similarly, students returning from serving Christ all day every day for months may well become vibrant members and leaders in their college churches. It is difficult to imagine hardly any dropping out. If mission adventures were to become normative, perhaps this would help mark the end of the mass exodus from church after high school.

Missions is evangelism and compassionate ministry in the name of Christ. Both here and there and to the uttermost parts of the earth. It flows from passion for Christ's renown and an insatiable thirst to see the multiplication of worshipers before His throne for all of eternity. On earth, the goal is not making converts but making disciples (Matthew 28:18–20). Or better yet, making disciple-makers among all peoples for the glory of God (2 Timothy 2:2).

CHAPTER 13

DISCIPLE-MAKING

By Richard Ross

Go therefore and make disciples of all the nations.
—Matthew 28:19a

For the glory of God, in the power of the Spirit, youth ministry makes disciples who make disciples among all peoples. Through His Great Commission, Jesus does not charge the church to make converts but to make disciples.

Definitions

Trying to draw a distinction between *Christian* and *disciple* is an error. Discipleship expert Bill Hull notes:

> The common teaching is that a Christian is someone who by faith accepts Jesus as Savior, receives eternal life, and is safe and secure in the family of God; a disciple is a more serious Christian active in the practice of the spiritual disciplines and engaged in evangelizing and training others. But I must be blunt: I find no biblical evidence for a separation of Christian from disciple. ... Believing without discipleship isn't believing, it's agreeing to a set of facts about a religious figure.[202]

---

[202] Bill Hull, *The Complete Book of Discipleship: On Being and Making Followers of Christ* (Colorado Springs, CO: Navpress, 2006), 33, 43.

Duffy Robbins says it this way: "Talking about a genuine conversion that isn't manifest in genuine discipleship is like talking about a genuine birth that isn't followed by genuine life."[203]

Youth pastors need a crystal-clear understanding of the terms *disciple* and *discipleship*. That understanding must begin with the biblical period. Robbins reports, "Clearly, back in the first century when the New Testament was written, the word was used to refer to adherents or followers of a great master—not just a teacher-student relationship, but a master-follower relationship."[204] Hull adds that, "A disciple, *mathetes*, is a learner or follower—usually someone committed to a significant master."[205] That Greek word for disciple, *mathetes*, is used 269 times in the Gospels and Acts.

Careful students of the Bible have drawn complementary definitions of *disciple* and *discipleship* from the Scriptures:

> **Michael Wilkins**: "A disciple of Jesus is one who has come to Jesus for eternal life, has claimed Jesus as Savior and God, and has embarked upon the life of following Jesus ... the process of becoming like the Master."[206]
>
> **Dallas Willard**: "The disciple or apprentice of Jesus, as recognized by the New Testament, is one who has firmly decided to learn from him how to lead his or her life, whatever that may be, as Jesus himself would do it. And, as best they know how, they are making plans—taking the necessary steps, progressively arranging and rearranging their affairs—to do this."[207]

---

[203] Robbins, *Building a Youth Ministry*, 79.
[204] Ibid., 77.
[205] Hull, *Complete Book of Discipleship*, 32.
[206] Michael J. Wilkins, *Following the Master: A Biblical Theology of Discipleship* (Grand Rapids, MI; Zondervan, 1992), 40, 42.
[207] Willard, *Divine Conspiracy*, 291.

Barry Sneed and Roy Edgemon: "Discipleship ... is a lifelong journey of obedience to Christ which transforms a person's values and behavior, and results in ministry to one's home, church, and in the world."[208]

Robby Gallaty: "So what is disciple-making? We could say that it is intentionally equipping believers with the Word of God through accountable relationships empowered by the Holy Spirit in order to replicate faithful followers of Christ."[209]

Leaders impact the lives of teenagers through many roles. This chapter gives primary attention to two of those roles—leading open Bible study groups and discipling teenagers in covenant groups. Even though these two groups are secondary to the home, they are vital Kingdom activity.

Open-Group Bible Study

Most churches provide an open-group Bible study for teenagers. Some provide two or more. The expression *open group* simply means any teenager can attend a group with no commitment and no expectations. The most common open groups meet on Sunday mornings, and they have names similar to Sunday School, Bible Study Fellowship, etc. A second open group each week may meet on Sunday evening, Wednesday evening, or some other time.

Open Groups Are Vital

When led well, open groups are strategic and vital to the church. Consider these values:

---

[208] Barry Sneed and Roy Edgemon, *Transformational Discipleship* (Nashville, TN: LifeWay, 1999), 3.
[209] Robby Gallaty, *Growing Up: How to be a Disciple Who Makes Disciples* (Bloomington, IN: CrossBooks, 2013), 19.

1. They frequently present how teenagers can begin a relationship with Jesus. They present the Gospel and they invite teenagers to become followers of Christ.
2. They teach new believers foundational concepts of discipleship.
3. They present the plumb line of God's Word to the largest number of teenagers.
4. They spiritually deepen teenagers in preparation for covenant discipleship groups.
5. They assist new teenagers with building a sense of belonging and community.
6. They introduce teenagers to adults who care for them and who are alive for Christ.
7. They provide a positive experience for teenagers whose families visit the church.

Every teenager needs an open-group leader who is living out and communicating truth, who is inviting teenagers into deep prayer, and who is providing care and ministry. When the Christ-centered life and teachings of this leader amplify and reinforce the voice of parents, a powerful discipleship synergy is formed.

Open groups are a *vital* part of youth ministry. Churches who have boring open groups should give concerted attention to waking up those groups to Christ and to creating stimulating group sessions. They should provide the best curriculum available. They should budget to provide quality training for leaders. Statements from the pulpit should communicate to teenagers and parents the high value of this youth ministry strategy.

Teaching for Change

Veteran youth ministry professor Ken Coley notes, "Where there is effective teaching, there is change—in knowledge, in perspective, in attitudes, and ultimately, in behavior. Where there is no change, no teaching and learning has occurred."[210] Effective open-group Bible study transforms the heart as the first step toward life change. According to Willard:

> The will, or heart, is the executive center of the self. ... It, more than anything else, is what we are.[211]
>
> [T]he greatest need you and I have—the greatest need of collective humanity—is *renovation of our heart*. That spiritual place within us from which outlook, choices, and actions come has been formed by a world away from God. Now it must be transformed.[212]

For decades, the goal of most youth classes has been to lead teenagers to understand and then apply the Bible. Understanding and application are part of the process, but leaders often skip the step that must come in between. Change in a believer's heart precedes outward change. "The good man out of the good treasure of his heart brings forth what is good; and the evil man out of the evil treasure brings forth what is evil; for his mouth speaks from that which fills his heart" (Luke 6:45).

Bible study that always makes a beeline to the glory and kingship of Jesus leads to heart transformation that *then* leads to application and changed behavior. Therefore, the flow of Bible study becomes:

1. Motivation.
2. Examination.
3. Adoration.
4. Application.

---

[210] Ken Coley, *Teaching for Change: Eight Keys for Transformational Bible Study with Teens* (Nashville, TN: Randall House, 2016), 6.
[211] Willard, *Divine Conspiracy*, 80.
[212] Dallas Willard, *Renovation of the Heart: Putting on the Character of Christ* (Colorado Springs, CO: Navpress, 2002), 14.

Ken Coley suggests eight principles that tend to lead to transformational Bible study:

1. Effective teachers assist their students in the process of comprehending new information and building God's truth into their thinking and behavior.
2. Effective teachers build on the prior learning experience of their teens.
3. Effective teachers engage their learners.
4. Effective teachers make use of different techniques in order to meet the diverse needs of their teens.
5. Effective teachers are aware of their own thinking and model this for their teens.
6. Effective teachers skillfully design cooperative learning activities so the results are positive and productive.
7. Effective teachers include brief assessments that provide evidence of student learning.
8. Effective teachers create a lesson plan that leads to transformation.[213]

Coley's book *Teaching for Change: Eight Keys for Transformational Bible Study with Teens* amplifies each of these principles and should be required reading for every youth leader.

Covenant-Group Bible Study

The complement to open groups is covenant groups. Covenant groups provide discipling relationships that involve more commitment and deeper relationships. Group members are those who have made a formal commitment to the process. First, that commitment might be communicated by an interview with the

---

[213]Coley, *Teaching for Change*, i, 5, 38.

youth pastor (or some other leader). This warm, affirming visit might focus on at least two issues:

1. Is it the general intention of your heart increasingly to know Christ, adore Him, discover more of His truth, and then follow His ways?
2. Is it the general intention of your heart increasingly to glorify Christ, to see His Kingdom come on earth, and to make disciples among all peoples?

Second, the teenager makes a commitment to the discipling process by signing a simple covenant. Bill Hull notes,

> A covenant that group members agree to will provide solid structure. A covenant speaks about specific expectations, such as attendance, participation, and arriving on time. ... The group's covenant works only to the extent that people establish relationships and bond to one another. Love and support provide the strongest form of accountability.[214]

Differences

Open groups and covenant groups are complementary but different youth ministry strategies:

- Rather than the foundational discipleship of open groups, covenant groups are built around deeper concepts and spiritual disciplines (Hebrews 5:12).
- Rather than open-group teaching about how to meet Christ, covenant groups presuppose teenagers know Christ and now want to become conformed to His image (Romans 8:29).

---

[214] Hull, *Complete Book of Discipleship*, 235.

- Rather than most study being done during the meeting times of open groups, teenagers in covenant groups usually are accountable for preparation and spiritual disciplines outside of meeting times.

Not only are covenant groups open to new members, but adding a new member should be their default perspective. Leaders might keep an empty chair present in every group meeting. This allows the leader to ask, "What new or long-term believer should be sitting in this chair? Who will pray and ask the Spirit to reveal that name to us?"

Groups focused on incorporating others are less likely to become prideful or exclusive. Rather than thinking, "I'm special," teenagers need to think, "I'm so grateful for where Christ is taking me, I want the same for every member of our youth group."

Covenant-Group Leaders

Current covenant-group leaders may know of adults who have potential to lead groups. With proper approval, current leaders might invite an adult to serve as an apprentice with them. As the group adds new members, the apprentice then can take two or three teenagers to begin a new group. Without a clear plan for beginning new groups, covenant groups may tend to become complacent about adding new members.

Churches that do not provide covenant groups simply group together teenagers at many different levels of spiritual motivation. Unfortunately, teenagers who want to go deeper in Christ tend to remain quiet about that desire. And they tend to just blend in with more shallow peers. They are hesitant to pray out loud with passion or to share deeper spiritual insights.

Only in covenant groups do they find the freedom to pray deeply and express themselves with others on a similar journey. Over time, such freedom may give teenagers boldness to more fully express their faith to the broader youth group.

In covenant groups, adults disciple teenagers of their gender. Discipling is different from teaching a class. Disciplers need to engage in accountability discussions that might touch on sexual issues. Disciplers may need to provide transportation for teenagers, meet them for coffee, connect at school activities, or visit in their homes. This degree of closeness between an adult and teenagers calls for same-gender relationships.

Size

The covenant-group model presented in this chapter focuses on one adult and around three teenagers in a discipling relationship lasting at least one school year. This discipling model mirrors the intensive investment Jesus made in Peter, James, and John.

What one-on-three disciplers are doing is biblical and effective, growing disciples through relationships while sharing life. They are following the example of Paul, who reported, "Having so fond an affection for you, we were well-pleased to impart to you not only the gospel of God but also our own lives, because you had become very dear to us" (1 Thessalonians 2:8).

Pastor and discipling pioneer Robby Gallaty reports, "So what is the ideal size of a [discipleship group]? In my experience, four total, as displayed by Jesus, is the number of choice. Any more than five, including you, is too large, and any less than three is too small."[215]

Veteran discipler Greg Ogden would agree: "My conviction is that the primary way people grow into self-initiating, reproducing, fully devoted followers of Jesus Christ is by being involved in highly accountable, relational, multiplying discipleship units of three or four."[216]

An adult discipler who goes into the world of a teenager shows that teenager he or she is valuable as a person, not just a church statistic. But going to a sporting event or band concert takes time.

---

[215] Gallaty, *Growing Up*, 47.
[216] Greg Ogden, *Transforming Discipleship* (Downers Grove, IL: InterVarsity Press, 2003), 54.

Deep conversations with lots of listening take time. Walking together, life on life, takes time. Adults who have their own jobs and their own families cannot make that kind of investment in more than three or four.

Even leaders who can visualize the value of covenant groups might be tempted to say, "With our current programs, we do not have enough adults engaged with our teenagers. How on earth will we find enough to lead covenant groups with only three teenagers in each?" That is a reasonable question.

Numerically, enough adults exist in most churches to lead covenant groups. But moving adults into new leadership roles will require fresh preaching, teaching, and discipling. Arm twisting, creating guilt, and shouting "ought to" has not worked and cannot work.

One of the most valuable roles of the senior pastor is calling out believers to serve. Pastors can proclaim from the pulpit that every Christ-follower is to have a ministry. He can challenge every adult small group to equip and send out members who will teach and disciple (not sit and soak).

Churches that only provide open Bible study groups and no covenant groups must consider some important questions:

- When youth ministry creates new spiritual hunger in a teenage believer, what comes next?
- When that teenager makes a conscious decision to become a disciple of Jesus, who begins to walk that teenager into a life of true discipleship?
- How do we dramatically increase the number of high school graduates who adore Christ, live out of gratitude for the Gospel, take responsibility for their own spiritual growth, articulate what they believe and why, know how to disciple others, sacrifice for the poor, live to take the Good News to the nations and the hard places in the U.S., and impact churches, business, entertainment, and government?

Covenant Group Meetings

Ideally, covenant group meetings should last a minimum of sixty minutes. None of those valuable minutes should be lost to late starts, announcements, music, or other activities. Sixty minutes just barely allows time to:

1. *Study Scripture* (30 minutes). Most groups likely will draw from biblically sound curriculum.
2. *Apply Scripture to life* (10 minutes). An open-group leader with many members has to fire scattered birdshot when it comes to application. The leader cannot possibly know what is weighing on the minds of so many. But someone who is walking life-on-life with only three can. One at a time, the leader can ask each teenager:

   - How does this Scripture give you insight into a situation in your life?
   - What way of moving forward seems most consistent with the nature of Christ as revealed in Scripture?
   - Last week, you shared with us your desire to move forward on a particular issue. How did that go? Is Christ nudging you toward a course correction as you continue to move forward?

3. *Plan for missions and evangelism* (5 minutes). Some plans will be unique to one covenant group, and some plans will bring together multiple groups. Hull notes, "If a group's world doesn't extend outside itself, the resulting selfish attitude can actually be destructive to the group members' faith."[217]
4. *Share warm, grace-filled accountability* (5 minutes).
5. *Pray deeply* (10 minutes). Perfunctory opening and closing prayers seldom draw teenagers into an actual

---

[217] Hull, *Complete Book of Discipleship*, 235.

conversation with the enthroned King. Including prayers that only are empty rituals prepares teenagers to become adults who will do the same for a lifetime. Ten minutes might be the absolute minimum time for every group member to pray aloud, offering praise to the Almighty, thanking Him specifically for His gracious acts, making heartfelt confession, committing to actions flowing from the Bible study, praying toward evangelism locally and globally, and (only then) praying for grandmother's gout.

Curriculum

A comprehensive content plan for covenant group discipleship is beyond the scope of this book. Some church leaders may be motivated to create such a plan, and some church leaders may choose to partner with publishers who have a plan that spans the six or seven youth ministry years.

A comprehensive plan might include solid Bible studies on core doctrines, the spiritual disciplines, interpreting Scripture, worldview, apologetics, marriage preparation, parenting preparation, male and female roles, identity in Christ, God's will, training in evangelism, training in missions, training in Christian leadership, training in service, training in discipling others, biblical morality, biblical relationships, and so on. Regardless of the topic, every study should:

- Immerse students in the truth of Scripture before considering human wisdom.
- Reveal facets of grace, the Gospel, and God's plan of redemption in that passage.
- Focus on heart change (knowing that is what leads to change in behavior).
- Exalt King Jesus.

Scripture Memory

Leaders who desire God's best will lead teenagers to memorize Scripture. Memorizing and reviewing passages will move truth into a teenager's long-term memory. That is what matters, not legalism or some church checklist.

Teenage disciples who memorize Scripture then can meditate (chew on it) anytime until it becomes part of who they are. After an extensive review of brain research, author Rick Yount concluded that believers become what they give continuing thought to. According to Yount:

> New thoughts, through concentrated attention, produce new behaviors. ... Through focused mental effort, by giving attention to this thought, not that, or this attitude, not that, or this action, not that, we actually change the structure and wiring of our brains. ... Focused attention, mental force, changes our brains to think God's revealed thoughts."[218]

These discoveries about the brain and mind add even more richness to such passages as:

- "Your word I have treasured in my heart, that I may not sin against You" (Psalm 119:11).
- "And do not be conformed to this world, but be transformed by the renewing of your mind, so that you may prove what the will of God is, that which is good and acceptable and perfect" (Romans 12:2).
- "Finally, brethren, whatever is true, whatever is honorable, whatever is right, whatever is pure, whatever is lovely, whatever is of good repute, if there is any

---

[218] Rick Yount, Presentation to the National Association of Professors of Christian Education, October 17, 2009.

excellence and if anything worthy of praise, dwell on these things" (Philippians 4:8).
- "Therefore if you have been raised up with Christ, keep seeking the things above, where Christ is, seated at the right hand of God. Set your mind on the things above, not on the things that are on earth" (Colossians 3:1-2).

Making Disciple-Makers

International missions leader David Platt declares, "From the start, God's simple design has been for every single disciple of Jesus to make disciples who make disciples who make disciples until the gospel spreads to all people in the planet."[219] Gallaty adds, "The expectation of Jesus and Paul was for every believer to make disciples—not some, not many, not most, but *all* believers. Being a Christian and making disciples are inseparable."[220]

When leaders picture a teenager being discipled by an adult, leaders usually picture the teenager in a receiving posture. But that is not the ultimate goal. Ben Trueblood reports, "Student ministry in large part has been content to spoon-feed Scripture and application of that Scripture to students rather than teach them how to study the Bible for themselves."[221]

As quickly as possible, a teenager needs to learn to take the initiative for his or her own spiritual growth. Today, many adults in the church have never begun to do that. Youth pastors cannot be content to produce even more adults in that condition. Beyond taking responsibility for their own spiritual growth, teenage disciples need to prepare to disciple someone else.

Most churches will experience more advantages when adults are included in discipling teenagers than when older teenagers alone disciple younger teenagers. *But adult leadership must not lead to teenagers who just sit and listen.* The goal of discipleship is not

---

[219] David Platt, cited in Gallaty, *Growing Up*, xvi.
[220] Gallaty, *Growing Up*, 29.
[221] Trueblood, *Student Ministry That Matters*, 55.

just making disciples. The goal is making disciples so enthralled with Jesus, so full of His aroma, and so expressive of His life that they make disciples. They become high school graduates who are motivated and equipped to disciple others in college, trade school, the military, the workplace, or the home.

Covenant-group members increasingly should take responsibility for leadership within the group.

- In middle-school groups, the adult may take primary leadership while the teenagers support.
- In younger high-school groups, the adult and teenagers may share leadership.
- In older high-school groups, the teenagers may do most of the leading while the adult supports.

Doubt

Some youth pastors might assume that doubt is only an issue for a handful of teenagers. They would be surprised to discover the vast majority of church teenagers have such thoughts. Powell reports:

> Seventy percent of the students in our study reported that they had doubts in high school about what they believed about God and the Christian faith, and just as many felt like they wanted to talk with their youth leaders about their doubts. Yet less than half of those students actually talked with youth leaders about them.[222]

God is not offended by honest questions. In fact, He welcomes them. Youth leaders and parents should follow His example. They need to rest in the confidence that the Christian faith as presented in Scripture is not going to collapse because one of their teenagers thought of a question.

---
[222]Powell, Griffin, and Crawford. *Sticky Faith*, 143.

Leaders show confidence that they believe the Christian faith is rock solid. But at the same time, they can humbly confess they do not have every answer on the tip of their tongues. Dallas Willard advises, "When we honestly don't know what to say at the time, we will just say so. We will go away and find an answer through study, conversation, and prayer."[223]

With humility in place, Willard advises that:

> We then listen prayerfully to those we teach. We encourage every question, and we make it clear that dealing honestly with the questions that come up is the only path to a robust and healthy faith. We never "pooh-pooh" difficulties, or take any problem with anything less than utter seriousness, or direct the slightest reproach or shame on anyone for having questions and doubts.[224]

Sometimes teenagers experience doubt after experiencing a moral failure. They may feel so guilty they begin to doubt their faith. The antidote to that is a more complete understanding of grace and the Gospel.

Parents and youth pastors can create an atmosphere that gives teenagers permission to express their doubts. They can walk beside teenagers as they press toward answers together. If they do, they will see many more young adults emerge from homes and churches with faith that lasts a lifetime.

The research is clear: "Most church teenagers doubt their faith. For a variety of reasons, few of them talk about those doubts. But those who feel most free to express doubts and discuss personal problems with youth leaders and peers show more lifetime faith."[225] Clark's study led to the same conclusion: "Safety to express doubt seems to be connected with stronger faith. We found that high

---

[223]Willard, *Divine Conspiracy*, 328.
[224]Ibid.
[225]Powell, Griffin, and Crawford, *Sticky Faith*, 143.

school seniors who feel most free to express doubt and discuss their personal problems with adults also showed greater faith maturity in college."[226]

Role of Youth Pastor

Biblical Illiteracy

One of the youth pastor's highest priorities is getting teenagers into the Word and getting the Word into teenagers. When a youth pastor first arrives at a church, he may well discover that even faithful teenagers know too little Scriptural truth.

- Chap Clark reports, "I'm convinced that the single most important area where we've lost ground with kids is in our commitment and ability to ground them in God's Word."[227]
- Barry Shafer adds, "The church today, including both the adult and teenage generations, is in an era of rampant biblical illiteracy."[228]
- Duffy Robbins takes this one step further when he says, "Our young people have become incapable of theological thinking because they don't have any theology to think about. ... And, as Paul warns us, this ... leaves us as 'infants, tossed back and forth by the waves, and blown here and there by every wind of teaching' (Ephesians 4:14)."[229]

Here is some good news: Churches that tend to produce teenagers who can articulate their faith do exist. The Study of Exemplary Congregations in Youth Ministry identified characteristics shared

---

[226] Clark, *Adoptive Youth Ministry*, 224.
[227] Chap Clark, quoted in Barry Shafer, *Unleashing God's Word in Youth Ministry* (Grand Rapids, MI: Zondervan, 2008), 13.
[228] Shafer, *Unleashing God's Word*, 14.
[229] Robbins, *Building a Youth Ministry*, 26.

by twenty-one churches that perennially are effective in youth ministry. Even across seven denominations, one shared characteristic that rose to the top was: "Bible study and biblical literacy are extensive and substantive."[230] Many more churches could become exemplary on this issue by giving it intentional focus.

The Youth Pastor as Equipper

Equipping the saints for the work of the ministry means assembling Bible teachers and disciplers weekly (or at least monthly). These gatherings can include joyful experiences of community, sharing the spiritual disciplines, and clarifying basic beliefs. The teenagers will be the beneficiaries of adults who are more spiritually alive and who comfortably articulate the truth of Scripture.

Few youth pastors have the time to meet weekly with open-group Bible study teachers and also meet weekly with covenant-group disciplers. Here is a creative weekly alternative: For about thirty minutes, the youth pastor equips, trains, and shepherds all adults who lead open-group Bible study and covenant-group discipleship. Then, the two groups divide, and for thirty minutes, they prepare specifically for teaching and discipling during the approaching session.

Once a month, parents can attend the first thirty minutes. This gives the youth pastor a consistent way to impact their walk with Christ and knowledge of Scripture. Then, during the final thirty minutes, a leader can provide guidance with specific parenting issues.

Such a plan means that, weekly (or monthly), the youth pastor spiritually impacts all the key adults in the lives of teenagers. All youth pastors are busy, but the equipping and transformation of these adults rises above other potential time commitments.

Please permit this personal note. When I was a 23-year-old youth pastor, a new church told me that youth leaders were "too

---

[230]Roland Martinson, Wesley Black, and John Roberto, *The Spirit and Culture of Youth Ministry: Leading Congregations toward Exemplary Youth Ministry* (St. Paul, MN: EYM Publishing, 2010), 84.

busy" and would not attend a weekly meeting. I decided to try. We met every week of the school year for twelve years. At my next church, the same scenario occurred. We met weekly for fifteen years. In my current church, I am a volunteer. As of this writing, I have trained our youth teachers and disciplers weekly for eight years.

The expression "too busy" is so vague it does not have meaning. People find the time to do those things that they value. People with many responsibilities attend weekly sessions for teachers and disciplers because:

- They can tell over time that they are falling more in love with Jesus.
- They love the laughter and joy with people who have become like family to them. Even though they may arrive tired out, they know they will leave with wind in their sails.
- They clearly can tell that their teaching and discipling is more transformational because they attend this hour.
- They love being prayed over and cared for when hard days come, especially if they have given up an adult class or group who would normally stand with them in a crisis.

The youth pastor is the key to these four elements. If he fails to infuse the meeting with one or more of them, his leaders probably will announce they are "too busy" to attend.

Preparing to Teach and Disciple
The youth pastor can train teachers and disciplers to use a six-day process when preparing a lesson.

Six Days Early
1. With your Bible, a journal, and your curriculum in hand, find a quiet place to meet God.

- Read the Bible focal passage for the session. Try to actually picture what is taking place in the Scripture.
- At this stage in the preparation process, you are focusing on yourself and your relationship with God.

2. If you have a curriculum that includes Bible commentary and background information on the focal passages, complete at least half of the Bible commentary on this day.

Five Days Early
1. Determine how this lesson fits into the unit and how it relates to the previous week's lesson.
2. Begin to memorize the key verse.
3. Pray for the students on your roll and for their lost friends.

Four Days Early
1. Complete the second part of the biblical commentary and background information.
2. Read through the main teaching plans of your curriculum to identify all possibilities.
3. Ask God to reveal to you what He wants and to specifically identify which of the teaching plan steps to use in your session.

Three Days Early
1. Complete the biblical commentary and background information.
2. Meet with or contact other teachers to find out what their thoughts are on the teaching plans and how they relate to students. Seek to discover what God has shown them through their study and preparation. Share ideas about how you are going to lead the coming session.

3. Call a student who shows leadership potential. Ask him or her to take part in the class by leading one of the teaching steps you are planning to use.

Two Days Early
1. Begin to finalize your teaching plans.
2. Continue to watch for ways that God desires to sharpen your walk based on the Scripture. Pray that God would go before you and work in the hearts of your students in preparation for the next Bible study.

One Day Early
1. Continue to pray that the Holy Spirit will move in your class. Pray that you will be able to recognize Him when He shows up so that you can help your students experience God in His living Word.
2. Think through the steps you have chosen to use in the session. Simply know the activities in the order you will use them and a couple of points you need to make sure are brought out during the activities.

Finding Teachers and Disciplers

Veteran youth leader and professor Chuck Gartman points to many different ways to identify leaders to teach the Bible and disciple teenagers:

1. Keep your eyes and ears open for adults who relate well to youth in other areas of church life.
2. Don't limit your search to younger adults. Look for potential leaders in unusual places such as the senior adult department.
3. Ask your current leaders for the names of persons who might be good youth leaders.

4. Check with your teenagers. See if there are people in the church whom they admire and would like to have working with them.
5. Parents are another source for discovering folks to work with youth.
6. Look over sponsor lists for youth activities. Many who are willing to go as sponsors on youth trips might also be willing to work with youth on a regular basis.
7. Study the rolls of adult Sunday morning Bible study classes to see who is active and faithful. There may be a person there who is waiting to be asked to work with your teenagers.
8. Consider having a church survey, in conjunction with other age groups, to discover potential leaders.[231]

Conclusion

Most youth pastors deeply desire to see believing teenagers transformed into the image of Christ. But new youth pastors may wonder if there are teenagers who desire that very thing. Experienced youth pastors know those teenagers do exist. And more exist than some adults would guess. Writing at age 18, Jaquelle Crowe is one of those teenagers:

> We've eaten the basics and are still hungry for more. We're ready for meat and reject the fluff so often pressed on us. We really don't want to be talked down to. We want to know how to live a godly life as teenagers and as Christians, and we don't want to be spoon-fed when we're ready to dig in ourselves.
>
> Why would we tackle the tough [meat] of truth when milk is perfectly acceptable? My answer: because we

---

[231] Adapted from Chuck Gartman and Richard Barnes, *Youth Sunday School for a New Century* (Nashville, TN: Broadman and Holman, 2001), 36.

love Jesus. If we love Jesus, we'll love truth, and we'll want to grow. We'll reject the status quo. These aren't our rebellious years; these are the years we rise up to obey the call of Christ. This isn't our time to slack off; it's our time to stand out. This isn't a season for self-satisfaction; it's a season for God-glorification.[232]

Hearing words such as these ought to motivate every leader to throw heart and soul into making disciples who make disciples.

---

[232]Crowe, *This Changes Everything*, 14.

Chapter 14

Worship and Prayer

By Richard Ross

Praise the Lord! Praise God in His sanctuary.
—Psalm 150:1a

Worship

"Worship is an active response to God whereby we declare His worth. ... To worship God is to ascribe to Him supreme worth, for He alone is worthy."[233] That active response to God includes the words, thoughts, attitudes, and actions of teenagers and their leaders.

The psalmist declares: "Ascribe to the Lord, O families of the peoples, ascribe to the Lord glory and strength. Ascribe to the Lord the glory of His name; bring an offering and come into His courts" (Psalm 96:7–8). And from the New Testament: "Worthy is the Lamb that was slain to receive power and riches and wisdom and might and honor and glory and blessing" (Revelation 5:12).

The goal is to see teenagers worshiping God with a sense of awe, in the spirit of Hebrews 12:28–29: "Therefore, since we receive a Kingdom which cannot be shaken, let us show gratitude, by which we may offer to God an acceptable service with reverence and awe; for our God is a consuming fire."

Teenage Christ-followers need a sense of connection with other believers. Jim Burns and Mike DeVries note that "although worship can be intensely personal, students best express worship in the midst of community. Worship is their chance to engage the

---

[233]Ronald Allen and Gordon Borror, *Worship: Rediscovering the Missing Jewel* (Eugene, OR: Wipf and Stock Publishers, 2000), 16–17.

living God in a personal way, in the midst of a community of others seeking His face."[234]

Allen and Borror add, "While it is true that worship is a state of heart, not of art, it is equally true that heart worship devoid of artistic expression is—to the extent it is deprived—impoverished. Heart worship is enriched by the arts. ... Art will not give birth to true worship, but true worship will give birth to artistic expression."[235]

Worship primarily is declaring the worth of God. But it also can change the worshiper. N.T. Wright adds, "Christian worship declares that Jesus is Lord and that therefore, by strong implication, nobody else is. ... It commits the worshiper to allegiance, to following this Jesus, to being shaped and directed by him."[236]

Burns and DeVries pass on these practical instructions concerning teenagers and worship:

- Teach what worship is and how to worship God.
- Help young people understand the characteristics and nature of God.
- Take the lead as a worshiper.
- Let the students plan and lead worship.
- Provide students opportunities to respond.
- Let students come as they are.
- Help students encounter the awesomeness of God.[237]

Whether or not the youth pastor leads in music worship, he can model the heart of a worshiper in front of the teenagers. Cole and Nielson tell youth pastors:

---

[234] Burns and DeVries, *The Youth Builder*, 122.
[235] Allen and Borror, *Worship*, 27.
[236] N.T. Wright, *Simply Jesus: A New Vision of Who He Was, What He Did, and Why He Matters* (New York: HarperCollins, 2011), 217.
[237] Burns and DeVries, *Youth Builder*, 123-25.

When you're in the front row singing at the top of your lungs, teenagers will follow your lead and discover the joy of singing praise to Christ. But when you're fiddling around with your message notes in the back or when you're talking to your volunteers during the singing, you're implicitly teaching teenagers that singing doesn't matter so much.[238]

Bottom line: Ushering teenagers into the throne room of heaven as they worship is an honor.

Preaching

Wise youth pastors construct sermons and talks that are text-driven and expository. Renowned preacher Charles Spurgeon said, "A sermon, moreover, comes with far greater power to the consciences of the hearers when it is plainly the very word of God—not a lecture about the Scripture, but Scripture itself opened up and enforced."[239]

Preaching professor David Allen adds, "Text-driven preaching is built on the solid foundation of the inerrancy and sufficiency of Scripture. Anything less than real exposition—which explains, illustrates, and applies the text to the people—does not reflect a proper view of biblical authority."[240]

Cole and Nielson note that expositional preaching has three main characteristics:

1. First, the sermon text is a single passage from Scripture, rather than various verses throughout the Bible.
2. Second, the theme of the expositional sermon is derived from the main point of the passage. … The

---

[238]Cole and Nielson, *Gospel-Centered*, 150.
[239]C.H. Spurgeon, *Lectures to My Students* (Grand Rapids, MI: Zondervan, 1972), 73.
[240]David Allen, "Text-Driven Preaching and Sermon Form," October 1, 2013, theologicalmatters.com.

goal is to proclaim what the biblical author intended to say to God's people back then in a contextualized, applicable way to God's people today.
3. Third, expositional teaching proceeds through an entire book of the Bible, from beginning to end, passage by passage. This enables you to teach each lesson in its proper biblical context, and to show how each individual passage supports the overarching theme of the entire book.[241]

David Allen adds that:

1. Text-driven preachers will do their exegetical homework to determine what the text means.
2. Text-driven preachers will engage in creative exposition to explain the meaning of the text to a contemporary audience.
3. Text-driven preachers will seek to become master communicators with an understanding of their audience and communication techniques that will make for the most effective preaching of Scripture with the goal of life transformation effected by the Holy Spirit.[242]

Worship and Hope in Christ

Worship can provide an antidote to the common thought, "My worship—just like all my faith—is all about me." Cole and Nielson point out, "It's good to sing about how we love God and need his help. But singing the word of Christ means singing songs that focus primarily on who Christ is and what he's done."[243]

---

[241] Cole and Nielson, *Gospel-Centered*, 55-56.
[242] David Allen, "Text-Driven Preaching and Pragmatic Textual Analysis," January 7, 2014, theologicalmatters.com.
[243] Cole and Nielson, *Gospel-Centered*, 144.

Furthermore, hope-filled worship transforms every other aspect of discipleship. Take, for example, missions. Worship among the nations is actually a preview of the coming time when people from every tongue, tribe, and nation will shout their redemption before Him who sits on the throne and before the Lamb (see Revelation 5:11-14).

True worship, therefore, must stir up in teenagers, parents, and leaders a greater determination to extend His praises among friends, neighbors, and unreached peoples. All evangelism is ultimately about expanding eternal adoration for God's Son into the midst of those who do not know Him.

The heart of every youth pastor should skip a beat when Rick Lawrence asks,

> Can you imagine the joy you'd taste if you could answer "adoration" when others innocently ask you what makes your ministry "successful"? Teenagers caught up in the pursuit and adoration of Jesus will live and breathe and move in the spirit of the first disciples—the same ones who started to believe that if they told a mountain to pick itself up and move, it would.[244]

Prayer

Concerning prayer, Greg Stier says:

> We need to pray. We need to help teenagers learn how to pray. We need to have regular prayer meetings and put more prayer into our regular meetings. When true intercessory prayer becomes the engine and not

---

[244] Lawrence, *Jesus-Centered*, 44.

the caboose of youth ministry strategies, we will see momentum in ways we never expected.[245]

According to Mike Higgs, "An effective prayer-driven youth ministry is one that is successful at creating a 'culture of prayer' both within and surrounding the ministry, so that participation in prayer becomes similarly pervasive."[246] Higgs believes this happens when at least six things happen:

1. The leader becomes a champion of prayer.
2. Students are mentored and mobilized in the area of prayer.
3. A designated prayer team is in place and functioning.
4. Ample opportunities are provided for everyone and anyone to participate in ministry-related prayer initiatives.
5. Students are the recipients of consistent, persistent, prevailing prayer.
6. Prayer infuses everything to the extent that the ministry is known as a praying ministry, just as the leader is known as a praying leader.[247]

Intercession for Future Youth Ministry

Ron Hutchcraft says, "The best plans do not begin in planning meetings; they begin in *prayer* meetings. ... [God] wants you broken on your knees and needing His power desperately. In that brokenness He will give you His dream. ... God gives the burden first, then the plan."[248]

Wise youth pastors organize prayer over planning sessions. They plan for concerted prayer before a group meets to set the youth

---

[245] Greg Stier, "A Gospel-Advancing," Kindle version.
[246] Mike Higgs, *Youth Ministry on Your Knees: Mentoring and Motivating Youth to Pray* (Colorado Springs, CO: NavPress, 2004), 89–90.
[247] Ibid.
[248] Ron Hutchcraft, *The Battleground for a Generation* (Chicago, IL: Moody Press, 1996), 57.

Worship and Prayer

ministry mission statement. And before setting the strategy. And before choosing programs and special events.

Youth pastors invite people to pray before those planning meetings are held, but they also call people to prayer in those meetings. One minute of opening prayer followed by fifty-nine minutes of human planning can never equal fifteen minutes of real prayer followed by forty-five minutes of Spirit-directed planning.

Church leaders talk about prayer. They teach that prayer is important. But sometimes the missing element is actually praying. A youth pastor might ask:

- What is our next major youth ministry event?
- About how many total man-hours have been invested in preparations for this event?
- About how many minutes or hours have believers spent interceding over this event?
- Are we placing more confidence in human preparations or the power of prayer in order to see Kingdom impact from this event?

The youth pastor should view a prayer strategy as crucial for every weekly program and every special event. This can lead the youth pastor to consider:

- How will teenagers, parents, and leaders be called to prayer in the weeks and days before the next event?
- How will the congregation be called to prayer? How will those in intercessory ministries know to pray?
- Who will pray immediately before the event and while it takes place? Who will pray over those with specific leadership roles in the event?

Teenagers Who Pray

Prayer over events matters. Teenage believers learning how to pray matters as well. Many youth pastors report that only a small percentage of their youth group is willing to pray aloud. Few seem to understand concerted prayer.

The Moral Therapeutic Deism that permeates church teenagers is on display when it is time to pray. When asked for prayer requests, the majority of teenagers respond only with the ways Jesus can give them what they want, take away what they do not want, and do the same for those they love. This should not come as a surprise because that is what they most often observe when they listen to their parents and other adults in the church.

A wise leader will say to teenagers:

1. Later, we will be praying for the sick and those with other problems.
2. But first, we are going to spend some time praying adoration to King Jesus. I want many of you to pray aloud, telling Jesus all the ways He is wonderful.
3. After that, we will pray prayers of thanksgiving.
4. Then, we will make confession through our prayers.
5. All that will prepare us to pray for the coming of Christ's Kingdom on earth, including the spread of the Gospel in your school and around the world.
6. We will close with prayer for the sick and those with other problems.

A spiritually alive youth ministry will lead to the disappearance of the statement, "Let me open us up with a quick prayer so we can get started." That expression has conditioned teenagers to look at their shoes for a few seconds and nothing more. Most would confess they do not pray during those brief moments. Also, that expression has conditioned teenagers to see prayer as a chore that must be completed before the event can begin rather than a part of the event itself.

Whether in open groups, covenant groups, or youth worship, when it is time to pray, it is time to actually pray. Those who lead Bible studies make preparation. Those who lead music worship make preparation. Those who call teenagers to prayer also should *plan* how to draw teenagers into actual conversations with King Jesus.

Teenagers develop a heart for prayer primarily through the modeling of parents and leaders. Those adults should put prayer at the top of their priority list. In a positive, grace-filled session, youth pastors might want to ask parents and leaders:

- What is your typical time and place for morning prayer? For prayer through the day?
- If teenagers were to observe your morning prayer, and just once you said those prayers aloud, would the hearts of those teenagers be warmed?
- When you pray with the teenagers you disciple, do your prayers cause teenagers to want to pray as deeply as you do? Do your prayers exude a passion to see Christ exalted as King of all for the glory of the Father in the power of the Spirit?
- When teenagers hear you pray, do they typically hear you intercede for specific people in your world who do not know Christ?

Prayer for Evangelism

As noted in chapter 12, researchers Rahn and Linhart report that youth ministries that routinely see teenagers reaching teenagers for Christ have adopted a God-dependent posture that centers on prayer. According to these researchers, "At the moment a student begins to interact with God for the sake of seeing another come to Christ, a change takes place."[249]

Greg Stier would say all this begins with the very heart of God:

> God has a heart for the teenagers in your community—a bigger heart than even you have! ... So when you engage in prayer for the lost, you tap into the mighty

---

[249]Rahn and Linhart, *Evangelism Remixed*, 88, 90.

river of compassion, mercy and love that flow through His divine veins, and a transfusion takes place in your heart and in the hearts of your teenagers.[250]

Prayer as a Part of Youth Ministry Gatherings

Public prayers have a biblical place in corporate worship gatherings. One complement to public prayers is small-group prayer. Since teenagers tend to have shorter attention spans, most can feel more engaged in prayer that directly involves them.

Even in very large venues, leaders may say, "Please stand and quickly form a small group with three or four around you. If you do not pray out loud, you may remain silent while the others in your small group pray aloud. Speaking in sentence prayers, I want you to adore the majesty of the Son of God until you hear the music begin."

Large worship gatherings likely will include teenagers who do not yet have a relationship with Jesus Christ. Will small-group prayer offend them? Not likely. In fact, this generation of teenagers is fascinated with spiritual practices. Even if they do not participate, pre-Christians may be intrigued as they listen to others speak to the Son of God in a personal way.

Prayer Room

The youth pastor can consider creating a permanent prayer room in the youth ministry area at church. Since chairs are optional, a floor covering can make sitting or kneeling comfortable. A permanent kneeling rail can face a focal point. Those who gather need a simple way to turn on instrumental worship music. Each wall can represent a different focus for prayer. For example, one wall could feature a floor-to-ceiling map of the world and could be the focus for global praying.

String and clothespins running the length of a wall can hold prayer requests and answers as well. Leaders can provide Bibles,

---

[250]Stier, *Gospelize Your Youth Ministry*, 76.

printed prayer guides, and art supplies so teenagers can express and display insights that come in prayer.

Additional Suggestions

1. When groups gather to pray, invite them to pray on one theme at a time. (For example: Adoration, Confession, Thanksgiving, and Intercession). Ask each person to pray aloud many times, but briefly each time. When a petition is offered, invite one or two others to pray in agreement with that petition.
2. When someone shares a prayer request with the group and then later offers prayer over that issue, this takes twice as much time. Invite group members to not share prayer requests with the group. Instead, ask them to begin praying aloud about their concern. Assure them the group will care about the issue and several will agree with them in prayer.
3. Teach teenagers, parents, and leaders the difference between prayers of praise and prayers of gratitude. Because of the current crisis in Christology, many believers do not know how to compose expressions of praise and adoration.
4. Show prayer groups how to find verses that capture what they want to say to Jesus, and then to pray those Scriptures aloud to Him.
5. Remind teenagers, parents, and leaders that church chairs have no seat belts. Invite them to stand, keel, or fall prostrate before the very Lamb of God.
6. When teenagers come to you one-on-one with a prayer request, they may be thinking you have an inside track with God that gives your prayers more power. You might respond to their sharing by saying something like, "I want you to know I care you are facing this challenge. But in reality, I'm just human

and I don't have the power to bring change to this situation. But King Jesus does. So, just begin now expressing your concern to Christ. After you have prayed, then I will join in and will express agreement with your desire to see Christ glorified in the situation." This approach teaches teenagers in any life challenge they should approach Christ first rather than last.

Every believer knows prayer is important. At the same time...

> Prayer itself is not the answer. Christ is the answer.
> The power is not in prayer itself.
> The power is in Christ.

But because prayer is conversation and union with the Triune God, its importance cannot be overstated.

Chapter 15

Community

By Richard Ross

Day by day continuing with one mind in the temple, and breaking bread from house to house, they were taking their meals together with gladness and sincerity of heart.
—Acts 2:46

Christ absolutely adores His Father and enjoys a deep relationship with Him. That is what He wants His followers (including the teenage ones) to taste with each other:

> "I do not ask on behalf of these alone, but for those also who believe in Me through their word; that *they may all be one*; even as You, Father, are in Me and I in You, that they also may be in Us, so that the world may believe that You sent Me. The glory which You have given Me I have given to them, that *they may be one*, just as We are one; I in them and You in Me, that they may be perfected *in unity*, so that the world may know that You sent Me, and loved them, even as You have loved Me" (John 17:20-23, emphasis added).

But for youth group members at church, such unity may or may not be happening. A Pew research study found that only 21 percent of teenagers say they spend time with their closest friends at church.[251] Reacting to that study, researcher Andrew Zirschky says:

---

[251] Andrew Zirschky, *Beyond the Screen: Youth Ministry for the Connected but Alone Generation* (Nashville, TN: Abington Press, 2015), 36.

Certainly, we encounter teenagers who fill our youth rooms and find themselves surrounded by their closest friends, but it's likely these teens are a minority, an oddity even. For the average American teenager, it is possible that going to church entails being surrounded by vague acquaintances and distant friends.[252]

But in reality, the body of Christ has embraced fellowship from the very first hours of the Christian church. "They were continually devoting themselves to the apostles' teaching and to fellowship, to the breaking of bread and to prayer" (Acts 2:42). The Greek sometimes translated "breaking bread" might better be translated "shared a pizza and two sodas."

A youth pastor reading this book might say, "I am fascinated and thrilled about focusing my youth ministry on the glory of Christ. I can hardly wait to launch deeper discipleship and I want to mobilize teenagers to care for hurting people. I better ditch anything that looks like fun and games."

Throwing the proverbial baby out with the bathwater is a mistake. Fellowship and building community only become negative in youth ministry when they get out of balance or are provided without purpose.

A few youth pastors believe they can provide fun for teenagers only if it quickly leads to some noble purpose. Christ might reply He delights in watching His kids find joy—period. Christ sacrificed His life, in part, so believers can experience joy together—"I came that they may have life, and have it abundantly" (John 10:10b). Joy is a fruit of the Spirit (Galatians 5:22).

Peer Relationships

Kenda Dean says every teenager who walks into the youth room carries three longings:

---

[252]Ibid.

1. Know me (the longing for communion).
2. Move me (the longing for transcendence).
3. Be there for me (the longing for fidelity).[253]

Each of those longings requires genuine relationships within the youth group.

Relationships are related to a life of discipleship. Kara Powell and her team of researchers found:

> Specifically, when we asked young people about church friendships, those who report more close friends at church also show higher faith maturity. As the number of close friends gets closer to five, so does the likelihood that a young person attends church and regularly participates in worship with others, takes time to read and study the Bible, talks openly with other Christians about their faith questions or struggles, serves others in need locally and/or globally, and sees their faith as an influence in their friendships.[254]

Lyman Coleman was an early pioneer in understanding how relationships impact discipleship. Jim Burns and Mike DeVries have provided a summary of Coleman's four levels of relationships, using the analogy of a baseball field. His model moves from a simple, nonthreatening level and grows toward a deep sense of belonging and trust.

First Base—History Giving. "Who am I?" This level deals with the facts about the person and his or her general history.

---

[253] Kenda Dean, quoted in Mark DeVries, *Sustainable Youth Ministry* (Downers Grove, IL: InterVarsity Press, 2008), 164–65.
[254] Powell, Mulder, and Griffin. *Growing Young*, 176.

Second Base—Sense of Warmth and Affection. "I am cared for and valued." When teenagers begin to know one another's stories, they begin to have a sense of acceptance. When teenagers feel cared for and accepted, they will begin to open up.

Third Base—Deeper Sharing. "I feel safe here." As teenagers feel safe and begin to share deeper issues, they need to be part of a community that continues to be unconditional.

Home Plate—the Depth of Christian Community. "I belong here." Within this level, teenagers are connected deeply with one another. This level is characterized by a sense of belonging so deep that teenagers see this grouping of people as family. These relationships can have an eternal impact on their lives and the decisions they make.[255]

Burns and DeVries summarize by saying: "Outstanding youth ministries proactively and purposefully move students through all four levels. ... Small groups are the vehicles that can get students to the level of community that their soul longs for."[256]

Intentionally Building Community

Since teenagers hunger for genuine friendships, leaders may wonder why most youth groups struggle with this issue. Veteran youth leader Jeanne Mayo has an answer:

> The root of most unfriendliness and cliquish behavior in today's youth culture is not self-centeredness or sinfulness. Rather, it primarily stems from students' personal awkwardness and insecurity when it comes

---

[255] Burns and DeVries, *The Youth Builder*, 101–3.
[256] Ibid., 103.

to initiating new friendships. ... If we truly believe that intentional friendship is a significant tool needed in youth ministry, we have to invest significant time in creating an atmosphere that makes initiating and cultivating friendships feel natural.[257]

Mark DeVries thinks at this point you have to become intentional. He reports, "Our youth ministry team decided we wanted to make our group the safest, most welcoming place in the city for teenagers, a place where no one could ever walk away saying 'I could never be cool enough' to fit in there."[258]

Of course, this is not something adults can do alone. Mayo says the first step is to give teenagers ownership of creating a new atmosphere. She notes, "I have never once taken a rental car for a wash, oil change, or mechanical checkup. Why? ... I don't care enough about the car to bother taking care of it. I have no sense of ownership. ... Your students need desperately to own this whole concept of making your youth group meetings more visitor-friendly."[259]

Approximately 20 percent of the youth group establishes the spiritual and emotional climate for 80 percent of the group. Mayo says, "Determine who the 'kingpins' are in the different demographic segments represented in your group. ... Share with them your desire to make sure everyone feels included in the youth group. Then bluntly ask for their help. Teenagers respond positively when we choose not to come across as the leader and instead humbly ask them to be on our team."[260]

Once some teenagers step forward to change the relational atmosphere of the youth group, youth pastors invest adequate time training them to know what to do. Then they can join in

---

[257] Jeanne Mayo, *Thriving Youth Groups* (Loveland, CO: Group Publishing, 2005), 68.
[258] DeVries, *Sustainable Youth Ministry*, 162.
[259] Mayo, *Thriving Youth Groups*, 34.
[260] Ibid., 76-77.

creating an environment where teenagers are treated with love and respect, and where visitors as well as faithful members are treated as valuable family members.

Youth pastors construct a warm and safe place where teenagers can stretch, experiment, try out new roles, and generally grow toward adulthood. Circles of friends who begin to love and trust one another tend to grow in discipleship more quickly.

Sarcasm

A major threat to that kind of atmosphere is the use of sarcasm by youth pastors. Mayo says, "Sarcasm is usually a measure of truth wrapped in barbing humor at someone else's expense. I've known many 'cool' youth leaders who have become specialists at communicating with teenagers through sarcasm. Ironically, the students they feel the most connected to are often the ones who get the brunt of their verbal jabs."[261]

Kurt Johnston and Tim Levert add:

> Using words as a weapon of mass destruction instead of tools for edification and encouragement may be the biggest hindrance to true community in your youth group. ... When teenagers are afraid to be themselves for fear of being picked on, or hesitant to share their thoughts for fear of being ridiculed, or generally feel like others are quick on the draw with a sharp word, why would they ever take the risk of sharing a genuine hurt, fear, or struggle?[262]

Over time, for good or ill, a youth group will begin to reflect the personality and the practices of the youth pastor. Mayo says, "We teach what we know, but we reproduce who we are. ... Your youth ministry will gradually begin to mirror your own conversation style.

---

[261] Ibid., 121.
[262] Kurt Johnston and Tim Levert, *The Nine Best Practices for Youth Ministry* (Loveland, CO: Group Publishing, 2010), 124.

With that in mind, it is absolutely imperative as a leader that you train your mind to search for positive things about everyone you meet."[263] Consider Ephesians 4:29: "Let no unwholesome word proceed from your mouth, but only such a word as is good for edification according to the need of the moment, so that it will give grace to those who hear."

Unity in Diversity
Christ has the ability to build unity among diverse teenagers.

- "For through Him we both have our access in one Spirit to the Father. So then you are no longer strangers and aliens, but you are fellow citizens with the saints, and are of God's household" (Ephesians 2:18-19).
- "If we walk in the Light as He Himself is in the Light, we have fellowship with one another, and the blood of Jesus His Son cleanses us from all sin" (1 John 1:7).

Researcher Andrew Zirschky believes the constant attention most teenagers give to social media reveals much about their relationships. He says, "The rise and dominance of social technology is a signpost that should help us see that teenagers are hungry for continuous, meaningful relationships with other humans and a kind of community not easily discovered in the disconnected landscape of modern American existence."[264]

Zirschky then adds these important points (paraphrased):

1. Teenagers use social media to establish "full-time intimate communities" that provide for always-on communication and relationships. Such communities differ significantly from the communities that

---

[263] Mayo, *Thriving Youth Groups*, 126.
[264] Zirschky, *Beyond the Screen*, 5.

teenagers experience daily in highly mobile (and consequently disconnected) face-to-face society.[265]
2. In an always-on-the-go society, these "always-on" relationships of persistent presence are what young people are seeking. And it is these that point to an even deeper yearning for a relational presence that is transcendent—a hunger for communion with God and others.[266]
3. Teenagers no longer derive their primary identity from one group. Rather, they have relationships with individuals whom they encounter through various groups. Their relationships are set within a network that is diffuse and sparsely knit—with vague, overlapping, social, and spatial boundaries. Many of the people they deal with do not know one another.[267]
4. Building a network is not a one-time endeavor. Teenagers must keep the network alive by making themselves engaging, interesting, and attractive, lest their network audience lose interest and slip away.[268]
5. The burden to craft a personal network and the possibility of losing their network community can ultimately mire young people in fear and anxiety.[269]
6. Fail to please the audience and you might find yourself without an audience. Lose the audience and you have lost your network. Lose the network, and at some level you lose the community that affirms and creates your very identity.[270]
7. Teenagers long for relationships of depth. Such a community of presence is precisely what the church is called by God to be and to offer to humanity. The

---

[265] Ibid., 13.
[266] Ibid., 36.
[267] Ibid., 55.
[268] Ibid., 67.
[269] Ibid.
[270] Ibid., 107.

New Testament word for such a community is *koinonia*, which can be translated as fellowship, sharing, or most poignantly, communion.[271]

8. The church is called to embody *koinonia*, an alternative operating system that delivers teenagers from the fear induced by maintaining a network. In *koinonia*, belonging does not depend on personal effort.[272]

9. In the communion of Christ, teenagers are meant to receive love and belonging when they have no social value, and they in return are invited to give love without considering the social value of others.[273]

10. Online practices should not replace offline interactions, but they can enhance and extend the communion experienced together. By learning to use social media in ways consonant with the marks of Christian communion, teenagers are formed in the alternative social operating system of *koinonia*.[274]

Community and Discipleship

God hardwired human beings for relationships. It should come as no surprise that most life-altering discipling takes place in the context of relationships. Spiritual transformation is as much caught as taught, especially where teenagers are concerned.

Relationships with Disciplers

Jim Burns and Mark DeVries say it this way: "Students need role models of what Christianity looks like lived in the context of life's issues. They need to see a model, not a perfect one but one that can show them the way."[275] Michael Wilkins adds that "a life-oriented approach to discipleship is so important. Jesus took

---

[271] Ibid., 6.
[272] Ibid., 67.
[273] Ibid., 70.
[274] Ibid., 146-47.
[275] Burns and DeVries, *The Youth Builder*, 27.

a small group of disciples with him in the various circumstances of life that he encountered on a day-to-day basis. He was able to provide an example for the disciples in all of the activities of life."[276]

Wise disciplers often invite their teenage disciples into their homes. Being a godly single, spouse, or parent in the presence of impressionable teenagers is powerful discipleship. Other rich venues for discipleship are the adult's workplace, the teenager's workplace, the teenager's extracurricular activities, and recreation conducive to conversation. Jesus certainly sat and taught some of the time, but mostly He discipled while sharing life with the apostles.

Wise disciplers deepen relationships with the parents of their disciples. If the door is open, disciplers almost become part of the family. They build a sense of partnership with parents, and they demonstrate they are worthy of trust. For parents who do not know Christ, introducing them to Him always is the goal. Seeing consistent, positive interest in their children can open the hearts of parents to the Gospel.

Community in Very Small Groups

In a typical Bible class of six to fifteen, teenagers tend to share at a superficial level. Mostly they try to give factual answers to questions asked about the lesson. If they are asked to share something personal, they keep their answers safe and light. Why? They have not built strong enough heart connections with the teacher or the teenagers to give them courage to share at a deep level. The teenager may have grown up with those in the classroom, but that does not necessarily mean heart connections and trust are deep.

Over time, a godly adult and about three teenagers can find that level of trust. They can make commitments of confidentiality. They can offer one another grace-filled accountability. They can make a covenant to watch out for one another. When teenagers begin to talk about their real thoughts, their real doubts,

---

[276]Wilkins, *Following the Master*, 142.

and their real lives, then the door is open for true discipling and lifetime transformation.

Teenagers often live lives marked by chaos and pain. They benefit from having a time and place to express what presently is making life hard. When they express those challenges, they need to hear from a compassionate leader and from compassionate peers who know them well. And they need prayer from those close by. Teenagers take time to express a concern, hear compassionate and biblically sound responses, and receive targeted prayer. Multiplying that time by more than three may leave no time for other discipling activity.

The Youth Pastor

Youth pastors long to see their teenagers love God, love people, and make disciples of all nations for the rest of their lives. Wise youth pastors know that building biblical community among the teenagers accelerates the accomplishment of that goal.

But the youth pastor's "congregation" is broader than just teenagers. The youth pastor also pastors parents of teenagers, the teachers and disciplers of teenagers, youth ministry sponsors, and the paid youth staff. The youth pastor shepherds his flock as he intentionally builds fellowship and community:

- Between teenagers and parents.
- Among the parents.
- Between teenagers and the adults who serve with them.
- Among the adults who serve with teenagers.
- Between the parents and the adults who serve with teenagers.
- Between teenagers and children in the congregation.
- Between teenagers and adults in the congregation.

When those groups of believers adore Jesus, then living together in biblical community makes it more likely they all will love God, love people, and make disciples of all nations—for the glory of King Jesus.

Chapter 16

Youth Ministry Leaders

By Richard Ross and William David Villarreal

He gave some as apostles, and some as prophets, and some as evangelists, and some as pastors and teachers, for the equipping of the saints for the work of service, to the building up of the body of Christ.
—Ephesians 4:11-12

Biblically, the role of an overseer is to organize and equip the people of God to do the work of God. This includes the youth pastor. One of the specific purposes of pastors is presented in Ephesians 4:12—"the equipping of the saints for the work of service, to the building up of the body of Christ."

A Biblical Example

The simple, biblical principle here for all pastors is: You cannot do it alone. This lesson is what God had to teach Moses. In Exodus 18, as Moses sat alone to judge or shepherd the people, his father-in-law Jethro revealed the need to more efficiently oversee his people:

> "The thing that you are doing is not good. You will surely wear out, both yourself and these people who are with you, for the task is too heavy for you; you cannot do it alone. Now listen to me: I will give you counsel, and God be with you. You be the people's representative before God, and you bring the disputes to God, then teach them the statutes and the laws,

and make known to them the way in which they are to walk and the work they are to do.

"Furthermore, you shall select out of all the people able men who fear God, men of truth, those who hate dishonest gain; and you shall place these over them as leaders of thousands, of hundreds, of fifties and of tens. Let them judge the people at all times; and let it be that every major dispute they will bring to you, but every minor dispute they themselves will judge. So it will be easier for you, and they will bear the burden with you. If you do this thing and God so commands you, then you will be able to endure, and all these people also will go to their place in peace" (Exodus 18:17-23).

The cause of burnout in ministry easily is seen here in the terms "wear out" and "too heavy." Jethro knew that the heavy burden would be too much for Moses to carry alone. Just as Moses had to train others to minister to God's people and help carry that heavy burden, youth pastors must equip youth leaders to help carry the important burden of making lifetime disciplemakers.

Volunteers or Leaders

Some churches use the term *volunteer* to refer to those who serve in youth ministry unpaid. But that term may not be best. Doug Fields says, "I prefer the word *leader* over *volunteer*. I like *leader* because it connotes action and affirms the value of the leader. *Volunteer* communicates that someone is needed to fill a slot no one else wants; it isn't as positive as *leader*."[277] Consistent with Field's thinking, this book uses the term *youth leader* rather than *youth volunteer* to refer to those with ongoing responsibilities in youth ministry.

---

[277] Fields, *Purpose-Driven Youth Ministry*, 274.

Finding Leaders

According to Fields:

> Some youth workers ask, "Why must I be selective about volunteers in the church? Isn't anyone who loves God and cares about students a qualified candidate?" No. We would be foolish not to show discernment with *all* potential hands-on leaders. If you are a leader of leaders, you must have a set procedure and criteria for selecting leaders. Your decisions in this area are far too important to your youth ministry to be made without a predetermined process.[278]

Moral Therapeutic Deism

When adults are full of Moral Therapeutic Deism, arm-twisting and telling them they "ought" to lead teenagers will fall on deaf ears. Before their hearts will embrace Kingdom service, they must move from "God exists for me" to "I exist for God." Such a transformation will have many facets, but the two most important may be these:

1. *Leading believers into a Christ awakening.* David Bryant says, "A Christ Awakening takes place whenever God's Spirit uses God's Word to reintroduce God's people back to God's Son for ALL He is. ... Whenever Christians wake up to fresh hope, passion, prayer, and mission focused on the full extent of the supremacy of Christ, they are seen to rise up to serve the King of glory in whole new ways."[279]

---

[278] Ibid., 290.
[279] David Bryant, "Why Our Mission Is so Critical," July 20, 2014, proclaimhope.org.

2. *Leading believers to experience overwhelming gratitude for the Gospel.* "The Spirit of God uses the beauty of the gospel to awaken in our hearts a desire for God. 'We love Him,' the apostle John would say, 'because He first loved us' (1 John 4:19 NKJV). Love for God grows out of an experience of the love of God."[280]

One of the most valuable roles of the senior pastor is calling out believers to serve. Pastors can proclaim from the pulpit that every Christ-follower is to have a ministry. He can challenge every adult small group to equip and send out members who will teach and disciple (not just sit and soak).

Potential Leaders

Adults in the congregation who are spiritually alive and emotionally healthy should be considered potential youth leaders. Potential leaders need to share four characteristics:

1. They need a walk with Christ that is alive and growing.
2. They need the capacity to offer unconditional love to teenagers that is warm and safe.
3. They need to comply with church policies related to background checks and waiting periods.
4. They need to have an identity grounded in who they are in Christ. There is no place for adults who want to have their needs met by teenagers or by the status of being a leader.

Identifying new leaders is one of the primary roles of the youth pastor. This responsibility is not confined to one season of the year. Every week he looks for the next leaders who will join the youth ministry team.

---

[280] Greear, *Gospel*, 11-12.

Enlisting Leaders

Wise youth pastors prepare a packet that includes everything potential leaders need to understand about serving in youth ministry. Chap Clark provides a description:

> The volunteer packet potentially includes: a welcome letter; an overview of what students need in a caring adult; the purpose statement and values of the church and ministry; general job descriptions; the involvement steps; the application; and a request for references and background check. Healthy teams have clearly established roles, responsibilities, and expectations.[281]

Hallway or parking lot conversations at church are not the place to enlist new youth leaders. Such a plan implies that serving is not that important and that little thought is given to potential candidates. Wise youth pastors make an appointment to sit down with the potential leader for unhurried conversation and prayer. A completed application gives the youth pastor details that help him direct the leader to a position that is a good fit.

Spiritually and emotionally healthy potential leaders generally are fine with background checks, waiting periods, and supplying references. Adults who are toxic may push back on such policies and thus disqualify themselves.

Pastoring Leaders

When enlisting a new leader, the youth pastor can announce, "I have a strong calling to disciple and equip leaders for youth ministry. Not only am I inviting you to give; I am inviting you to receive. As you become part of the youth ministry leadership team, I will pour into you and invest in you in ways that will matter

---

[281]Clark, *Adoptive Youth Ministry*, 286.

the rest of your life." Of course, such pronouncements only have value if they are truthful.

Chap Clark agrees with the need for such investment: "In your youth ministry community, you will likely discover that volunteers are working through their own formational and personal challenges. Youth pastors, then, must pastor their volunteers as much as they pastor their [teenagers]."[282]

The most powerful way to see youth ministry goals fulfilled is to spiritually transform parents. With few exceptions, children will become who their parents are today. But the second most powerful way to see those goals fulfilled is to give teenagers heart connections with adults:

- Who love God with all their heart, soul, mind, and strength.
- Who love others as they love themselves.
- Who value the glory of God above all things.
- Who are ready to live or die as they join majestic Christ in bringing His Kingdom on earth.

Paul told Timothy, "The things which you have heard from me in the presence of many witnesses, entrust these to faithful men who will be able to teach others also" (2 Timothy 2:2). Following that same principle, youth pastors disciple adults so they will be prepared to disciple and lead teenagers.

Joining Christ in deepening adults takes time. It takes time to invest in them one-on-one, and it takes time to bring them together. Some youth pastors might say, "Well, that's a nice idea, but I would never have the time to do those things." That is like a fireman who is too busy to fight fires or a surgeon who is too busy to operate.

Spiritually alive and growing adults produce spiritually alive and growing teenagers. What is more important than that? Youth pastors who honestly do not have the minutes to invest in adults

---

[282]Ibid., 325.

need to cut back on activities or need to allow teams to handle preparation for events.

Youth pastors should consider these thoughts:

- Do you believe disciplers tend to have deeper relationships with teenagers when they have been in their homes? Then be in the homes of the adults.
- Do you want adults to attend the games and performances of their teenagers? Then offer to have lunch with adults or support their activities.
- Do you want adults to share a cup of coffee with a teenager who is in a hard place? Then invest one-on-one time with an adult going through a tough period.

Pre-Service Training

Youth pastors train teachers, disciplers, and leaders before they begin leading teenagers. Attention should be given to interpreting Scripture, spiritual disciplines, the curriculum that will be used, group dynamics, understanding teenagers, and intercessory prayer.

The Youth Pastor as Seminary

The youth pastor should be a seminary for his leaders. In other words, he should pass on to his leaders most of the important content he learned while at seminary or in other training and study. Cole and Nielson say, "It is wrong, in fact, for us to keep whatever skills we have in teaching and preaching to ourselves. We should share them, for the good of those we train and for the salvation of all they will reach."[283]

Potential leaders might meet weekly for a school semester before they begin their service. Inviting leaders to commit to thirteen weeks of training and spiritual growth attracts strong leaders, and it filters out those who cannot keep commitments. Among other possibilities, such training could be offered during the Sunday

---

[283] Cole and Nielson, *Gospel-Centered*, 133.

morning Bible study hour. The thirteen weeks might include such topics as:

1. The goal of youth ministry.
2. Expectations and commitments for leaders.
3. The Gospel.
4. Principles for interpreting the Bible.
5. Principles for teaching the Bible.
6. Spiritual disciplines.
7. Spiritual gifts—yours and your teenagers'.
8. Understanding teenagers' inner world.
9. Understanding teenagers' outer world.
10. Teenage crises.
11. Family crises.
12. Partnering with parents.
13. Tracking youth culture.

Wise youth pastors who lead such training say they want to teach new leaders most of what they know about youth ministry. Clark adds:

- "Make sure volunteers understand what 'faithfulness' looks like in the youth ministry. Do not assume volunteers know what you mean....
- "Make sure you explain to your volunteers what they need to do and what they don't need to do. Some volunteers attempt to do too little, while others attempt to do too much."[284]

The youth pastor and the leaders can make the decision to raise the bar on expectations for leaders. Low expectation leads to low performance. A covenant the leaders sign may be the visible representation of the raised bar.

---

[284]Clark, *Adoptive Youth Ministry*, 326.

When the youth pastor trains leaders, he should model high-quality education, the high quality he expects from the leaders. He should not use a lecture to teach them not to lecture. He should teach in view of the various learning styles, just as he hopes they will.

Spiritual Impact on Leaders

Churches today often place adults who never have been intentionally discipled in leadership roles with teenagers. Youth pastors ask adults to create a transformative small-group experience when adults never have been part of a group that did more than listen to "the lesson." Spiritual lethargy does not generate transformation, and adults cannot create what they never have seen.

As noted in chapter 13, the church is in an era of rampant biblical illiteracy. This state of affairs means that pre-service training must include instruction in how to interpret the Bible correctly. New leaders may very well receive such instruction for the first time in their lives. Cole and Nielson add, "First and foremost, my conviction is that training for God's people needs to be explicitly *Word* training. The first priority for students is increasing their ability to competently read, study, understand, and apply the Word of God."[285]

Youth pastors impact adults during gatherings at church and in one-on-one time together. They also impact adults during special events. One of those events might be a retreat. Youth pastors value youth retreats because they remove distractions, allow teenagers to hear God, and open up space for reflection and deep conversations about faith. Adults stand in great need of those same things. Occasionally, it may be more strategic to take just the adults on a retreat—knowing their future impact on the teenagers will not be the same.

The principle is the same related to out-of-town conferences. Bringing home a van of adults whose hearts have been warmed may be the first step toward new spiritual life in the entire youth

---

[285] Cole and Nielson, *Gospel-Centered*, 132.

group. In addition, the youth pastor should develop a resource library where leaders can seek further instruction. This can include books, media, magazines, or anything pertaining to youth ministry.

Regular Gatherings of Leaders

If youth pastors want to see teenagers grow in Christ, they have to take intentional steps in that direction. If youth pastors want to see adult leaders grow in Christ, they also have to take intentional steps in that direction.

Weekly Meetings
As noted in chapter 13, weekly or, at the very least, monthly gatherings of adult leaders are essential for consistent spiritual growth. A youth pastor should prepare for these gatherings with the same care as a youth group meeting.

Gatherings allow adults to go new places in prayer. Rather than serving as a meaningless ritual, prayer may well take a fourth or more of the meeting time. This allows the youth pastor to show leaders how to offer prayers of pure adoration and praise and to create an atmosphere of grace that permits confession. And that provides time for heartfelt thanksgiving. And that allows space for intercession—praying for the coming of Christ's Kingdom, praying for teenagers by name, praying for the leaders' families, and praying for one another.

The youth pastor also can use gatherings as a time to build community among the leaders. As an expression of the body of Christ, this is a time for adults to enjoy one another, to laugh and cry together, to care for one another, and to gently nudge one another toward growth.

This does not always have to be at church. Allowing adults to enjoy a movie or an evening in someone's home may be more valuable than yet another youth activity. Adults who have discovered authentic community with one another are likely to create that same community among the teenagers they lead.

Youth leaders should come to see this time as their primary discipleship experience through the church. They should see this time not as a meeting but as the gathering of a community that is valuable to them. They should believe serving in youth ministry and attending such gatherings has added value to their lives.

Meeting Content

The meetings themselves should allow new leaders to *experience* a rich group gathering. What they observe and experience can shape the gatherings they plan for teenagers. A session might include:

1. Celebration of spiritual victories.
2. Problem-solving related to issues or crises arising in the groups.
3. Examination of future teaching content.
4. Continuing training in how to interpret Scripture.
5. Continuing training in how to build relationships and to disciple.
6. Experiencing spiritual disciplines and accountability.
7. Intercessory prayer for the disciplers and the teenagers.

As noted in chapter 15, both open-group (Sunday School, etc.) leaders and covenant-group leaders can be included in the meeting. They have the same need for spiritual growth and accountability. They have the same need to receive spiritual leadership from the youth pastor. Covenant-group leaders and open-group leaders can meet together for spiritual growth and then separate to focus on their unique curricula and meeting plans.

Conclusion

Pastors, parents, and leaders can be a chord of three strands in the life of a teenager. As those adults intertwine their respective ministries, they likely will see:

Teenagers who, for the glory of the Father
and in the power of the Spirit,
spend a lifetime embracing the supreme majesty of the Son,
responding to His majestic reign over all of life,
inviting Christ to live His life through them,
and joining Him in making disciples among all peoples.

Chapter 17

Planning and Administration

By Richard Ross and Roy Michael Kelly, II

*Without consultation, plans are frustrated,
but with many counselors they succeed.*
—Proverbs 15:22

What factors are central to effective youth ministry that leads to lifetime faith? To answer such questions, Kara Powell's research team conducted surveys, interviews, and site visits with churches across the U.S. They soon discovered that the following ten qualities are *not* necessary for churches to have life-altering youth ministries:

1. A precise size.
2. A trendy location or region.
3. An exact age.
4. A popular denomination ... or lack of denomination.
5. An off-the-charts cool quotient.
6. A big, modern building.
7. A big budget.
8. A "contemporary" worship service.
9. A watered-down teaching style.
10. A hyper-entertaining ministry program.[286]

If those factors are not what makes a difference, then what does? This book answers that question with several core concepts:

---

[286] Powell, Mulder, and Griffin, *Growing Young*, 25-27.

I. The three arenas for youth ministry are:
   a. Ministry with the families of teenagers.
   b. Ministry with teenagers and the full congregation.
   c. Ministry directly with teenagers.

II. The functions of youth ministry are:
   a. Worship.
   b. Evangelism.
   c. Discipleship.
   d. Ministry.
   e. Community.

III. The primary outcomes of youth ministry are:
   a. Love God.
   b. Love people.
   c. Make disciples of all peoples—all for the glory of God.

Concepts to Action

But those concepts are just that—concepts. Youth pastors must lead a process that moves youth ministry from concepts to action. Nehemiah can serve as their example in that process. Nehemiah wanted to restore the home of his heritage. His goal was to rebuild the wall surrounding Jerusalem and, more importantly, to bring his people back into a right relationship with God.

Nehemiah's plan began with prayer and claiming the promises of God. Nehemiah 2:5 records a conversation in which Nehemiah said to King Artaxerxes: "If it please the king, and if your servant has found favor before you, send me to Judah, to the city of my fathers' tombs, that I may rebuild it."

Nehemiah had a clear goal, and he knew the elements necessary to complete that plan. The elements included a timeline, requisition of resources, travel plans, and sponsorship. Once in

Jerusalem, his plan included covertly surveying the previous wall placement, developing resources (people as well as financial), and reestablishing holiness in the temple and in the hearts of the residents, all while dealing with adversity.

Nehemiah used strategic thinking in his planning. He accomplished his goal of rebuilding the wall in just fifty-two days. The words "strategic plan" are not found in the book of Nehemiah, but the evidence is there: a goal was set, and tasks and resources were aligned to achieve the goal. Problems arose, deadlines came and went, but Nehemiah's spoken goal of rebuilding the wall was accomplished. Youth pastors can be equally successful as they move through a planning process.

The Planning Process

The following is an overview of the planning process:

1. Lead a Purpose Statement Design Team to define a purpose statement for your youth ministry.
2. Lead your youth ministry to own the purpose statement.
3. Design a concrete way for teenagers, parents, and leaders to evaluate present youth ministry in light of the purpose statement.
4. Create a Core Planning Team to shape your plan for the coming year.
5. Guide the Core Planning Team to digest the concrete evaluation of youth ministry.
6. In light of that analysis, guide the Core Planning Team to set several high priorities for the coming year.
7. Choose ministry responses (programs, events, ministries, etc.) to those high priorities, being careful to identify a primary youth ministry function and target audience for each.

8. Move the ministry responses you have chosen to twelve balanced, monthly calendars.
9. Create Lead Teams to implement each major programming element.

A Purpose Statement

Creating a youth ministry purpose statement (or mission statement) takes vision. Tim Smith says, "Vision is a specific mental image of what God wants to accomplish through you to build His Kingdom. ... Vision comes from God. God supplies the vision."[287] And, Smith adds, "Growth is more likely to occur in youth groups where there is a specific description of what they are trying to accomplish."[288] Paul, one of the greatest visionaries in the Bible, said, "I press on toward the goal for the prize of the upward call of God in Christ Jesus" (Philippians 3:14).

A Purpose Statement Design Team usually is a small group of core teenagers, parents, and leaders who are spiritually transformed and sensitive to the Spirit's leading. Ideally, they know how to see the big picture and they are motivated to craft a statement that sets the direction for their youth ministry.

Doug Fields has laid out an excellent approach to defining a purpose statement:

1. Work with the pastor and other church leaders to clarify the direction your church is heading so the youth ministry purpose statement will work in harmony with it.
2. Teach the biblical foundation for the five youth ministry functions to the team shaping the purpose statement.
3. Invite the team to express their thoughts and to suggest words and phrases.

---

[287]Tim Smith, *8 Habits of an Effective Youth Worker* (Wheaton, IL: Victor Books, 1995), 66.
[288]Ibid., 69.

4. Compose the final statement.
5. If the church has a purpose statement, ensure the youth ministry purpose statement clearly flows from it.
6. Request support from the pastor for the new statement.
7. Launch the purpose statement with wisdom.[289]

Owning the Purpose Statement

Again, no one can improve on Doug Fields' suggestions for getting your new purpose statement into the DNA of teenagers, parents, leaders, and the congregation. Here is a brief summary:

1. Challenge key teenagers and adults to memorize the statement.
2. Teach on the statement and ask your staff to do so.
3. Make your statement visible with a poster or banner.
4. Print the statement on letters and calendars.
5. Review the statement at meetings of parents and leaders.
6. Show parents and church leaders that every program supports a purpose.
7. Invite each stakeholder in youth ministry to pray for one of the purposes.[290]

Evaluation of Present Youth Ministry in Light of the Purpose Statement

This might be a standardized evaluation from a publisher. Or, the evaluation might be notes from a "town hall" meeting with youth ministry stakeholders that solicited feedback. Finally, evaluation might be feedback from focus groups.

---

[289]Adapted from Fields, *Purpose Driven*, 60-66.
[290]Adapted from Fields, *Purpose Driven*, 71-75.

A Core Planning Team

The Core Planning Team usually is composed of core teenagers, parents, and leaders who are spiritually transformed and sensitive to the Spirit's leading, who have the purpose statement in their DNA, and who are adept at planning. Since the church has called the youth pastor to take the lead in shaping its youth ministry, he chairs this team.

As the team considers ministry to and with teenagers, having teenagers in the conversation is important. As the team considers the needs of parents, it makes sense that parents are on the team. As the team plans to empower and equip leaders in entirely new ways, the voices of some of those leaders need to be heard.

Youth Ministry Functions

Youth ministry and the full church share the same functions: community, discipleship, evangelism, ministry, and worship. Missions is the melding of evangelism and ministry.

Ministry Responses

Ministry responses are the events, programs, and ministries the Core Planning Team plans to address priorities for the year. Some programming will target specific subsets of teenagers, some will target parents, some will target leaders, and some will target the congregation. Some will target teenagers and their parents, some will target teenagers and their leaders, some will target teenagers and members of the congregation, and some will target leaders and parents.

Lead Teams

Imagine a youth pastor has been working long hours every week, coordinating a ministry just for teenagers and their leaders. Then, that youth pastor wants to move to a workweek that is more likely to lead to lifetime faith and Kingdom impact for most teenagers. The youth pastor becomes convinced that giving a third of a week to the families of teenagers and a third of a week to teenagers in the congregation is crucial to building such lifetime faith.

In such a scenario, an obvious question arises: How does the youth pastor find two-thirds of a workweek for these new arenas of ministry? Only one answer seems reasonable.

> The youth pastor must move away from spending large blocks of time planning and preparing for the next major event or trip.

Instead, he must equip the saints to take the lead role with event and trip preparation as they serve on Lead Teams.

Lead Teams serve to implement events or projects calendared by the Core Planning Team. Examples include youth camp, a retreat, an all-night prayer gathering, or a family remodeling project at the rescue mission. Lead Teams serve to implement events or projects according to a design and spirit affirmed by the Core Planning Team, and consistent with the vision and direction of the entire congregation.

Lead Teams are composed of teenagers, parents, and leaders. Lead Teams generally have four to twelve members. Lead Teams are assembled to prepare for a particular event or trip and exist only long enough to fulfill that objective.

Lead Teams should not be confused with groups or committees who "help the youth pastor" with an event. Lead Teams accept ultimate responsibility for their event or project. The youth pastor serves to motivate, inspire, and give general direction to their work, but the team has ultimate responsibility.

Teams do not do all the work on events and trips. They may involve many members in their work. They simply take the lead, coordinating role.

The Purposes of Lead Teams

The purposes of Lead Teams include:

1. To assist the youth pastor in moving to a leadership style that emphasizes equipping the saints to do the work of the ministry, in the spirit of Ephesians 4:11-12.
2. To enable the youth pastor to shift time from event and project management to his higher priorities.
3. To open opportunities for teenagers, parents, and leaders fully to express their callings and giftedness as they arise to join Christ in His Kingdom activity.

Chairpersons

The selection of the chairperson may be the most important variable in the effectiveness of Lead Team ministry. Chairpersons must be seasoned youth ministry leaders who have a clear vision of the events and projects they are creating. They must be fully supportive of the youth pastor and share his heart for ministry.

Meeting Times

Most churches will experience greater success when Lead Teams meet simultaneously. Several advantages exist:

1. The youth pastors can spend the entire time going team to team, offering encouragement, solving problems, and ensuring the quality of plans underway.
2. When teams meet at the same time, attendance is more visible and team members feel more accountable to attend.
3. Members feel more excitement when they see a larger number of team members at work.

Youth pastors need to protect a prime meeting time for Lead Teams, without conflicts. Monthly simultaneous meetings will be about right for most churches. Teams quickly approaching their event may decide to plan additional meetings or work sessions.

A team chairperson and the youth pastor should decide how many months before an event a team should begin meeting. Complicated projects such as an out-of-state mission trip may require a six-month head start. A simple activity at the church may only require two months.

Timeline

Churches can discover the best timeline for their situation. Here are three options:

1. Organize all Lead Teams for the year at the same time. After membership on all teams is set, announce when each team will begin meeting during the year (typically from two to six months before their event or project). Allow team members to rest after they complete their assignment.
2. Organize Lead Teams at the beginning of each quarter. Organize teams that will lead events not during that quarter, but in the quarter to follow. (For example, organize teams in September that will lead events from December to February or March.)
3. Assemble teenagers, parents, and leaders and organize a specific Lead Team when it is time for that team to begin meeting.

When considering the above options, the basic questions are: How long do we want team members to have off before we challenge them to join a new team? When they finish their work, do we want them to be off until the beginning of the new church year? Off until the beginning of the next quarter? Do we have so few youth and adults that we need them to begin a new team assignment right away? Each church's situation is different.

Budget Administration

Each Lead Team chairperson needs clear guidance on the money his or her team has to spend. The easiest way to communicate this is with budget line items for Lead Team events. Chairpersons quickly can see the amounts they have to spend. Since budget reports are public, chairpersons tend to take those limits seriously.

Quality Control

Youth pastors care about the quality of programming provided for teenagers, parents, and leaders. Watching something done poorly is painful. Leaders considering the Lead Team concept may honestly wonder: How do I know teams actually will do quality work?

Lead Teams do not come with guarantees. However, teams in scores of churches across the nation are indeed providing first-class events, activities, and projects. Most do not want to be associated with leading a flop. Much more importantly, most want to maximize their impact for the Kingdom.

Youth pastors can monitor the quality of planning in at least two ways. First, youth pastors can move from team to team during the regularly scheduled team meeting sessions. Visiting informally with a team provides some sense of how they are progressing in their plans. No team wants a third-degree interrogation, but light questions are not offensive and provide the feedback you need.

Also, youth pastors can stay in touch with chairpersons informally between scheduled team meetings. Church hallway conversations, phone calls, and even lunches together provide valuable feedback. Once again, no one enjoys an FBI-styled questioning. Instead, youth pastors can initiate conversations with questions such as, "Is there any information I need to get you about your retreat? Any help you need from me?" Gentle questions in the context of offering help and showing interest generally lead to the feedback the youth pastor needs.

Making the Case for Lead Teams

To motivate others to consider Lead Teams, youth pastors can make the following points during a group presentation to all teenagers, parents, and leaders:

> *A. The Bible suggests a better way for us to organize our youth ministry.*

The youth pastor can lead the group in a word-by-word study of Ephesians 4:11-12. He can use commentaries and Bible study tools to prepare a thorough study. He can emphasize that pastors are given gifts primarily to be used in equipping the saints so the saints can perform the work of the ministry. The youth pastor can explain there may be a way to organize youth ministry closer to the New Testament pattern.

> *B. There may be a better way to organize our youth ministry that would allow us to expand and move into any areas where we sense God is at work.*

The youth pastor can explain that with the present organization, adding new ministries is difficult. He may even want to say that because he is basically in charge of everything, he simply does not have time to consider adding new programs or ministries. He then can present the possibility there may be a way to organize that would allow the church to respond quickly to new needs and opportunities that emerge, and to begin new ministries in response to seeing where God is at work.

> *C. There may be a plan that would allow the youth pastor to move into new areas of ministry.*

Here the youth pastor can help the group see the need for him to begin spending more time in new areas of ministry or to expand the time in ministries that presently receive inadequate attention.

D. *Hundreds of churches are adopting a strategy that is New Testament in design, allows them to move into many new areas of youth ministry, and allows their youth pastors to give more attention to their highest priorities in ministry.*

At this point, the youth pastor can present the Lead Team strategy. He can adapt the strategy to fit the church's situation. He can use handouts and visuals to aid communication. Then he can allow open discussion and provide positive answers to questions that may arise. If the group seems open to the strategy, he can enthusiastically announce what the next step toward implementation will be.

Prayer

One of the most common and most dangerous statements made in the church today is, "Somebody please open us in a quick prayer so we can get started." For believers who are waking up to the supreme majesty of Christ, that statement ought to sound like long fingernails clawing an old blackboard. The statement is very close to saying, "Let's get this ritual over with as quickly as possible so we can get on with applying our human intelligence to planning good youth ministry."

Jesus prayed all night before He chose the first apostles. The youth pastor should pray a long time before enlisting the team that will shape the youth ministry purpose statement. The early church in Acts prayed deeply (and even fasted on occasion) before making major decisions. When teams convene, deep prayer should be a central agenda item.

Team members do not just lengthen the prayer time by taking prayer requests and then praying for grandmother's gout. They adore and magnify the Triune God. They confess sin. They proclaim gratitude for blessings. Then they cry out for wisdom to know the mind of Christ in setting a purpose statement for their youth ministry.

When that work is finished, the youth pastor goes back on his knees to discover whom Christ has chosen for the Core Planning Team. Then, he gives more time planning how they will pray than planning any other part of the agenda.

Later, when they complete the evaluation, the group thanks God for the insights He provided and then asks for wisdom for the next step. When they complete the priorities for the new year, they pause for more prayers of thanks and more prayers for the mind of Christ. When they complete each item of the agenda, the process is the same.

Later, every Lead Team should follow the same pattern. The youth pastor should be more careful to teach chairpersons how to lead group prayer than teach them how to lead a good meeting.

The Role of the Youth Pastor

The planning process described in this chapter immerses teenagers, parents, and leaders in the adventure. But shared leadership does not diminish the importance of the youth pastor to the process.

In all of the meetings, the youth pastor likely will have done the most careful study of Scripture related to the task. He may be the most widely read in the field and may have the most formal or informal training. His passion for Christ, for teenagers, and for youth ministry may motivate him to spend the most hours per week thinking carefully about this arena of ministry. In other words, he is extremely important to the planning process.

Shared leadership does not call into question the youth pastor's competence. In fact, it takes more competence to equip and guide the saints to craft youth ministry than it does to do unilateral planning in the office with the door closed.

Parent Advisory Team

Wise youth pastors give parents a way to speak into the design and execution of youth ministry. A Parent Advisory Team is one way to do just that. Such a team is not a decision-making team. Rather, team members serve to advise the youth pastor. Such a team might meet monthly during the school year. A Parent Advisory Team exists:

1. To help the youth pastor understand what churched and unchurched parents need.
2. To assist in designing ministry that meets the needs of those parents.
3. To plan how to equip and provide resources for parents to fulfill their God-given role as parents.
4. To consider how all elements of the youth ministry will be seen through the eyes of parents—and to recommend changes where needed.
5. To represent all parents, including those with both positive and negative voices.

A Final Challenge

Now you have seen a radically new model of youth ministry likely to lead many more teenagers to
lifetime faith.
Are you willing to give up
"comfortable" youth ministry in exchange?

PART 4

Epilogue

Chapter 18

The Youth Pastor

By Richard Ross

*One thing I do: forgetting what lies behind and
reaching forward to what lies ahead.*
—Philippians 3:13b

I was a youth pastor for almost thirty years.[291] Now I am a professor. I love teaching future youth pastors at Southwestern Seminary. In addition, by God's grace, I am out speaking almost every Sunday of the school year. Preaching and speaking on the road are a joy and a privilege. But if God told me to stop teaching and traveling and to again serve as a youth pastor, I would.

If a church were to call me as youth pastor, I would do some things, but I would not do one thing. What I would not do is have an all-night lock-in. As Hezekiah 6:66 clearly states, that idea has demonic origins.[292] Anything that leaves you feeling that badly the next day must be from the dark world.

The following are things I would do. They reveal how I view the position of youth pastor. If I became a youth pastor again, then:

I increasingly would love God with all my heart, soul, mind, and strength. By the Spirit, day by day, He would become my primary passion. My increasing love for Him would flow from my gratitude for grace and my celebration of the Gospel.

Since the Son is the clearest revelation of the Godhead in our day, I would adore Him as my King Regent, enthroned and ruling

---

[291] This section is an adaption of the Epilogue in the book: Richard Ross, *The Senior Pastor and the Reformation of Youth Ministry*.
[292] To clarify for the less biblically literate, this is not an actual book of the Bible.

over all things. I would move into deeper intimacy with Him as I look forward to the consummation of our relationship on new earth.

I increasingly would abide in Christ as I move through the day. I would stay in a running conversation with Him, marked by both awe and intimacy. I would enjoy Him while He enjoys me.

I would protect undisturbed time early in the morning to worship King Jesus. I would invite Him to speak to me through His written Word. I would sit in silence and listen for His voice. I would adore Him. I would intercede for people and Kingdom issues that seem to be on His heart.

Because of my morning worship and my abiding with Christ through the day, I would begin to think and act more as He thinks and acts. I increasingly would delight in that which delights Him, and I would grieve over that which grieves Him.

In the power of the Spirit, the Father's glory increasingly would become my consuming mission. I would glorify Him in our relationship and as I join Him in bringing His Kingdom on earth.

I increasingly would love others as I love myself. I would love deeply my brothers and sisters in Christ. I would love the lost nearby and in the nations. I would love those in need. I would join Christ in turning love into sacrificial action.

Daily I would saturate my mind with Scripture. I would allow that wisdom to define my thoughts and actions, my relationships with and leadership of my family, and all my approaches to ministry.

I would love individual teenagers in unconditional, grace-filled, and pure ways. I would expect nothing in return. I would use my words and hugs to bless, build up, and encourage each one. As I walk away from them, I would pray I leave behind the aroma of Jesus.

I would love individual parents and leaders in unconditional, grace-filled, and pure ways. I would expect nothing in return. I would use my words and hugs to bless, build up, and encourage each one. As I walk away from them, I would pray I leave behind the aroma of Jesus.

In partnership with other spiritual leaders, I would join Christ in leading parents to meet Him, supremely love Him, experience awe at His majesty, become much more transformed into His image, and join Him in bringing His Kingdom on earth. I would lead them to be transparent about their life in Christ and to spiritually lead their children in planned and spontaneous ways. I would provide specific ways for families to serve, perform the functions of the church, and accomplish the Great Commission locally and globally.

In partnership with leaders inside and outside our church, I would teach parents how to parent. I would guide them to desire the glory of Christ and His Kingdom as their highest goal in parenting. In order to see transformation and training in parenting, I would assemble parents at least monthly. I would allow ministry priorities to determine church schedules and not the other way around.

In partnership with other spiritual leaders, I would join Christ in leading youth leaders to meet Him, supremely love Him, experience awe at His majesty, become much more transformed into His image, and join Him in bringing His Kingdom on earth. I would lead them to be transparent about their life in Christ and to spiritually lead teenagers in planned and spontaneous ways.

In partnership with leaders inside and outside our church, I would teach youth leaders how to spiritually lead teenagers. I would guide them to desire the glory of Christ and His Kingdom as their highest goal in leadership. In order to see deep transformation and continual training in leadership, I would assemble youth leaders weekly. I would allow ministry priorities to determine church schedules and not the other way around.

In partnership with other spiritual leaders, I would lead members of the congregation to form heart connections with teenagers. I would lead all ages of adults to love individual teenagers in unconditional, grace-filled, and pure ways—expecting nothing in return. I would lead them to use words and hugs to bless, build up, and encourage each one, leaving behind the aroma of Jesus.

In partnership with other spiritual leaders, I would make changes to selected programs so that teenagers increasingly experience church in rich relationships with older and younger generations. I would give teenagers and adults ways to serve and perform the functions of the church side by side.

I would pair every teenager with an older, spiritually alive adult in a long-term prayer mentor relationship. I would lead teenagers to experience the full church as their spiritual family.

I would lead the church and families to provide rites of passage ceremonies for every 13-year-old. I would lead the church increasingly to see teenagers as young adults.

I would introduce teenagers to Christ. I would invite teenagers, parents, leaders, and the congregation to join me in introducing teenagers to Christ. In partnership with other spiritual leaders, I would train believers to share their faith in the power of the Spirit and with the joy of Christ.

In partnership with other spiritual leaders, I would challenge and invite many members of the congregation spiritually to prepare and then receive training to disciple teenagers. I would never stop until I had enough leaders to disciple teenagers in small groups.

I would disciple all teenagers in open Bible study groups. I would guide those groups to be evangelistic, to teach foundational discipleship concepts, and to create a sense of community.

I would identify teenage disciples with clear intentions to follow Jesus. I would form them into covenant discipleship groups composed of one or two leaders and about three teenagers. I would lead the leaders to disciple teenagers so those teenagers are prepared to disciple others the rest of their lives.

I would lead parents and leaders to ensure every teenager knows and understands the basics of the faith, provides a reasoned defense of the faith when needed, sees reality in ways consistent with Scripture, experiences the spiritual disciplines as an overflow of the heart, and increasingly thinks and acts like Jesus.

I would lead teenagers, parents, and leaders to pray deeply. Through Scripture and example, I would guide them to praise Jesus with awe at His glory and to talk with Him with warm intimacy. I would lead them to be extravagant in their thanksgiving. I would guide them to intercede for people and situations—primarily to see God's glory and the coming of His Kingdom, rather than asking for quick fixes for every situation.

I would lead groups of teenagers, parents, and leaders to intercede weekly over every element of youth ministry.

In partnership with parents and leaders, I would mobilize teenagers to take the Gospel to their families, schools, community, nation, and world. I would model and then lead them to make sacrifices for the sake of the Gospel. I would place them in challenging situations that move them beyond their comfort zones. I would call most young adults to spend weeks or months on the front lines of missions within a year of high school graduation.

In partnership with parents and leaders, I would mobilize teenagers to address human needs locally and globally in the name of Jesus Christ. I would model and then lead them to make bold sacrifices for the sake of those in need. I would place them in challenging situations that move them beyond their comfort zones.

I would assist other spiritual leaders in planning Sunday morning worship services. My goal would be to draw teenagers increasingly into the experience. I would lead teenagers to see this service as the primary weekly gathering of God's people.

I would provide a weekly worship service for teenagers. I would include the proclamation of Scripture, worship music, deep prayer, and experiences that build community. I would welcome lost teenagers. I would let them hear truth proclaimed boldly, let them observe the worship practices of passionate followers of Christ, and let them be loved in grace-filled ways.

Believing that many are wiser than one, I would bring together core teenagers, leaders, and parents to envision and calendar youth ministry events. I then would organize teams of teenagers, leaders, and parents to make each of those events happen. I would not get deeply involved in preparing for events so I could do those things unique to my calling as youth pastor—those things listed in this chapter.

In partnership with parents and leaders, I would provide events for teenagers that build community and reflect the abundant life. I would reveal to them that those who think and act like Jesus can experience exuberant joy unknown by the world. At times, that would include eating some pizza.

If I started over as a youth pastor, I am pretty sure that is what I would do.

Practical Advice for the Youth Pastor
By Richard Ross and Clayton Ross

1. Enlist an accountability partner. Every youth pastor needs someone who asks, "When was the last time you looked at sinful computer images?" "Which member of our youth group are you most likely to fantasize about?" "How are you doing with your plan to have a weekly date night with your wife?" You and your partner need to be direct with each other, but you also need to drench each other in the cleansing grace of the cross.

2. Your accountability partner needs access to any social media account you use to connect with teenagers. Every communication you have with a teenager should be accessible to that partner. Entirely private digital chats are as dangerous as meeting a teenager in your office at midnight.

3. Don't be alone with teenagers or adults of the opposite sex. Have a pane of glass installed in your office door. Don't ride in a car or share a meal with only one member of the opposite sex. Don't end up as the

last adult on the parking lot with a member of the opposite sex. If all this sounds too strict, you don't understand the world we live in. You need a mentor.

4. You can make a spiritual impact on a teenager, or you can have sexual fantasies about a teenager. But you absolutely cannot do both. Your choice will help you know the condition of your heart.

5. There is a clear line that two people cross that can lead directly to an affair. An "innocent" touch, a sentence with double meaning, or eyes that meet a second too long can be that line. Just decide that never in your life will you cross that line with a teenager or adult. Believing you can cross the line and later stop yourself in time is pure insanity.

6. If you don't want to follow the advice in points 1-5, then leave youth ministry. You have no right to cripple young lives because of deficits in yours. Maybe these lines are your wake-up call, and today you will enter biblical counseling, intense discipleship, and accountability.

7. Speak to every person you pass at church. Just decide you will never pass a single person without speaking. Because you are a leader, you speak first. You speak even when your greeting is not returned. You speak even to people who don't seem important to your ministry. You speak even if you are shy. When you pass someone without speaking, and you are a pastor, that person will be confused and probably will mention this to others, and your stock will trade lower.

8. Learn the names of senior saints. Greet them. Pop in on their luncheons (yum). Show interest in their world. Their attitude toward the youth ministry will be largely shaped by their contact with the youth pastor.

9. When people invest time, work, or money in your ministry, thank them. Every time. Publically and privately. Train the teenagers to do the same. Keep training until the teenagers get good at it.

10. Train the teenagers how to behave in a home. Hosts genuinely want the teenagers to be comfortable. At the same time, there is a sting when teenagers damage their home only because of acting badly.

11. Train the teenagers how to behave in a place of business. Every time a manager tells you how amazed he is with your group, pass that on to the teenagers.

12. Continually cooperate with the Spirit to become more humble. Arrogance is impossible to hide long-term. The unpaid leaders who are attracted to an arrogant pastor are not the adults you want around teenagers. Truly humble pastors attract really healthy leaders.

13. If you try to be a bigger deal than parents in the eyes of teenagers, be worried. If you dislike moving other leaders into the spotlight with the teenagers, be concerned. Using your leadership role to try and prop up a low impression of yourself is dysfunctional. Until you are comfortable in who you are in Christ alone, you may need to take a sabbatical for some healing.

14. Be humble enough to be discipled or mentored.

15. Never shout in anger at a misbehaving teenager. Never touch a teenager in anger. Parents will forgive about anything but this. No matter what the teenager was doing, your outburst will be the bigger infraction in the minds of the family, the youth group, and the congregation. If you have anger issues, you need to run to someone who can assist you.

16. Teenagers behave best when they know specifically what the consequence for misbehavior will be. "If you open your motel door one time tonight, I will immediately call your parents to drive the four hours to pick you up." "If your talking makes worship impossible tonight, you will be warned one time and then sent home. You will be welcome next week, but tonight you absolutely will be sent home."

17. Ensure teenagers see you with a strong work ethic. You are a role model. Let them see you work just as hard and just as focused as your peers in secular vocations.

18. Don't turn to teenagers to solve your personal problems. Go to people your age or a biblical counselor to talk about your romance woes, loneliness, church troubles, etc.

19. Make close friends with your own age group. Don't use teenagers as a crutch to avoid relationships. Let the teenagers see you doing church things with people your age.

20. Let teenagers and other adults see you honor and care for your family of origin.

21. If you are married, let your teenagers know you love your wife way more than them. Let them know you protect most of your evenings and portions of your weekend just for her. Be appropriately affectionate with your wife in public. Many of your teenagers have not seen a warm marriage.

22. If you are married, do not dump youth ministry duties on your wife just because you forgot something or failed to plan well.

23. If you are married, celebrate if your wife happens to be called to youth ministry. But equally celebrate if she is called to some other area of church life. When talking with search committees, clarify her calling and the fact that the church is not calling two for the price of one.

24. If you have children, let them know they are a higher priority than the youth group. Some of the time, take one or all of your children to youth events so teenagers can watch good parenting. Just don't overdo taking them.

25. Return texts in an hour or two, emails the same day, and calls the same day. Parents and leaders evaluate your competence in part based on your responsiveness.

26. Train your church to know that non-life-threatening calls and messages received in the evening will be returned the next morning. Handling messages in

the evening will burn you out and will greatly frustrate those you live with.

27. Sunday is a workday, and you need a Sabbath. Take a full Saturday or the equivalent of a Saturday as that day of rest. Do not "run by the office," etc. In addition, press hard to get at least three uninterrupted evenings a week. Otherwise, you will burn out and the people you live with will be damaged.

28. When you are considering major decisions or major redirections of ministry, go away on a prayer retreat. Deep prayer, Scripture searching, thinking, and reflection are impossible in your office.

29. If someone in the church doesn't like you, move toward that person rather than away. Go out of your way to speak. Try to carry on conversations. Avoiding the person just intensifies the problem and allows the person to imagine more things that may not be true. Just decide there will never be a person in the church that you go out of your way to avoid.

30. When someone has issues with you, and you feel certain you are the innocent party, you go to that person anyway. You go to his home with a humble attitude. You listen carefully and you beat down the normal tendency to defend yourself. You apologize for any offense, even if your motives were innocent. You listen for anything the person says that is true. When you hear of changes you need to make, you promise to address them. If the two of you cannot resolve some concrete issue, you agree to meet again with more interested parties.

31. With conflict at church, remember the iceberg. For example, you give a leader what you consider to be constructive criticism. He reacts with anger that seems too extreme for the situation. The top of the iceberg is your criticism. The bottom of the iceberg is the fact that he was repeatedly abused as a child, and anything that now seems to be mistreatment sets him off. Yes, you may need to address how you present negative feedback. But conflict will not be so confusing when you know some or much of it is coming from below the water line.

32. Remain curious to know how your early years shape your life now. Don't be absorbed, but be curious. You may not be responsible for things that happened to you while young. But you are responsible for getting insight into those things. And then healing through prayer, Scripture, and wise counsel. Most people go a lifetime without a clue, and therefore they continue to do things that harm their lives and ministries.

33. If you have been through more than one similar crisis in your present church, or across several churches, this probably is not a coincidence. You likely have a blind spot that is causing conflict without your knowing it. Ask those who know you best if they can see ways you are creating conflict or hurting others. If no one is willing to be that honest, invite a biblical counselor to assist you in gaining insight.

34. Never say to teenagers, "Anything you tell me will be held in complete confidence." Instead, say, "I will never share anything you tell me with anyone who is not part of getting you the help you need." Then, learn the laws in your state concerning reporting

statements made by teenagers that may indicate they are being abused, may hurt themselves, or may hurt others. Even when you are in doubt, you make the call to appropriate professionals. You never, ever decide you are sufficient to work things out. Or you will sit in bitter pain at some funerals.

35. Don't fail to replace a toxic leader just because you dread conflict. You are the shepherd and you protect your flock, regardless. The stress that accompanies removing a leader is less than the stress and harm that will come later if you do nothing.

36. Don't assume you always understand the teenagers better than their parents do. You only see a small slice of a teenager's life. And every expert will tell you that most teenagers are very different at home than at church. Welcome insights from parents who see another side of your teenagers.

37. Don't rush to take sides in conflict between teenagers and parents. Listen and learn from both. Remain objective. Be pastoral, regardless of your age. Be a peacemaker.

38. Go out of your way to have conversations with parents. Point out positives in their son or daughter. Your words will be music to their ears.

39. Don't give extra time and attention to the teenagers who are attractive or who build up your ego. The entire youth group will be very aware if you do. Love them all and bless them all. But give a bit of extra attention to the invisible teenagers and to those too empty to inflate your ego.

40. Unless your youth group is in the hundreds, seek to speak to every teenager every Sunday or Wednesday. Because your time with each may be limited, mostly bless and build up the teenager. After teenagers forget most of your programs, they will remember personal time you invested in them.

41. Sarcasm is toxic, even when teenagers bravely try to laugh. Sarcastic humor damages your impact on teenagers.

42. Never stop learning. Teenagers, youth ministry, churches, families, and the culture are complex and deserve clear thinking. If you cannot relocate, connect with the best formal training in youth ministry through live video. In your scraps of time, read. Attend conferences that best reflect your perspective on youth ministry.

43. As you choose what to do in professional development, give priority to what you are best at and what you are weakest at. What you are best at represents a great opportunity to make an impact in your church and even beyond. What you are weakest at will continually trip you up.

44. Genuinely build up the other pastors. Most unpleasant attitudes and leadership errors spring from feeling inadequate or inferior, so minister to that.

45. Do not talk negatively about the senior pastor. Period. No matter how "trusted" the person you talk to seems to be, your words will come back to haunt you. If the issue is the pastor's gross immorality,

then confidentially seek counsel from a denominational leader or trusted pastor in the area.

46. If the senior pastor has a blind spot that is impacting ministry, then very humbly offer to share insight with him on the issue. If he listens to you and then decides not to change, then drop the issue. Make your only discussions on the issue to God in prayer. Weaknesses and errors in the senior pastor are between him and God.

47. Every senior pastor has deficits. But some sins or errors rise beyond the typical. If your integrity will not allow you to stay and serve, then quietly prepare to leave. For example, if the senior pastor told you to prevent teenagers of other races from attending, that would be a hill to die on. You gracefully take yourself out from under his leadership, and you carefully seek not to harm the church in the process.

48. Never, ever fire a parting shot as you leave a church (i.e., broadcasting negative information not known by most of the congregation). Even if you have been treated terribly. Even if the pastor is adulterous. Even if "setting the record straight" would be temporarily satisfying. For one thing, you will become known as a leader who creates problems. Future search committees will toss your resume even though they don't know all the details. Even more importantly, protecting the bride of Christ is more important than your feelings.

49. Stay within your budget. Other leaders in the church consider overspending to be arrogant and a breach of trust with the congregation.

50. Every character in the Bible was a flawed, imperfect person. And yet God continually demonstrated His supernatural ability to bring Kingdom impact out of imperfection. Praise God for grace. Praise the Great Physician for healing. Praise the God of Second Chances who picks up leaders, dusts them off, and sends them back into the battle. Including you and me.

> And praise the King for considering you worthy
> to join Him in transforming teenagers
> to spend a lifetime loving God, loving people,
> and making disciples of all nations
> for the glory of God.

BIBLIOGRAPHY

Books

Allen, Holly Catterton and Christine Lawton Ross. *Intergenerational Christian Formation*. Downers Grove, IL: InterVarsity Press, 2012.

Allen, Ronald and Gordon Borror. *Worship: Rediscovering the Missing Jewel*. Eugene, OR: Wipf and Stock Publishers, 2000.

Anthony, Michael and Michelle Anthony. *A Theology for Family Ministries*. Nashville, TN: B&H Academic, 2011.

Bakke, O.M. *When Children Became People*. Philadelphia, PA: Fortress, 2005.

Barna, George. *Revolutionary Parenting*. Carol Stream, IL: Tyndale, 2007.

Barna, George. *The State of Youth Ministry*. Ventura, CA: The Barna Group, 2016.

Bergler, Thomas E. *The Juvenilization of American Christianity*. Grand Rapids, MI: Eerdmans, 2012.

Black, David A. *The Myth of Adolescence*. Maitland, FL: Davison, 1999.

Black, Wes. "The Preparatory Approach to Youth Ministry," *Four Views of Youth Ministry and the Church*, Mark Senter, ed. Grand Rapids, MI: Zondervan, 2001.

Blomberg, Craig. "Matthew," *The New American Commentary*, Vol. 22 Nashville, TN: Broadman and Holman Publishers, 1992.

Bryant, David and Richard Ross. *Christ Is All: A Joyful Manifestation of the Supremacy of God's Son*. Providence, NJ: New Providence Publishers, 2005.

Buchanan, Justin and Sarah Buchanan. "Raising Teenagers to Live on Mission for God." In *Everyday Parenting*, edited by Alex Sibley. Fort Worth, TX: Seminary Hill Press, 2017. 97-113.

Burns, Jim and Mike DeVries. *The Youth Builder*. Ventura, CA: Gospel Light Publications, 2002.

Cannister, Mark. *Teenagers Matter: Making Student Ministry a Priority in the Church*. Grand Rapids, MI: Baker Academic, 2013.

Carson, D.A. et al., eds., *New Bible Commentary: 21st Century Edition*. 4th ed. Downers Grove, IL: InterVarsity Press, 1994.

Chapman, Gary. *The Five Love Languages of Teenagers*. Chicago, IL: Northfield Publishing: 2000.

Clark, Chap, ed., "The Adoption Model of Youth Ministry," *Youth Ministry in the 21st Century: Five Views*. Grand Rapids, MI: Baker Academic, 2015.

Clark, Chap. *Adoptive Youth Ministry: Integrating Emerging Generations into the Family of Faith*. Grand Rapids, MI: Baker Academic, 2016.

Clark, Chap. *Hurt 2.0: Inside the World of Today's Teenagers Youth, Family, and Culture*. Grand Rapids, MI: Baker Academic, 2011.

BIBLIOGRAPHY

Cole, Cameron and Jon Nielson. *Gospel-Centered Youth Ministry*. Wheaton, IL: Crossway Publishers, 2016.

Coley, Ken. *Teaching for Change: Eight Keys for Transformational Bible Study with Teens*. Nashville, TN: Randall House, 2016.

Crowe, Jaquelle. *This Changes Everything: How the Gospel Transforms the Teen Years*. Wheaton, IL: Crossway, 2017.

Dean, Kenda. *Almost Christian*. New York: Oxford University Press, 2010.

Dean, Kenda, Chap Clark, and Dave Rahn, eds. *Starting Right: Thinking Theologically about Youth Ministry*. Grand Rapids, MI, 2001.

Dever, Mark. *Nine Marks of a Healthy Church*. Wheaton, IL: Crossway, 2004.

DeVries, Mark. *Sustainable Youth Ministry*. Downers Grove, IL: InterVarsity Press, 2008.

Dupee, Dan. *It's Not Too Late*. Grand Rapids, MI: Baker Books, 2016.

Epstein, Robert. *The Case against Adolescence: Rediscovering the Adult in Every Teen*. Sanger, CA: Quill Driver Books/Word Dancer Press, 2007.

Fields, Doug. *Purpose-Driven Youth Ministry: Nine Essential Foundations for Healthy Growth*. Grand Rapids, MI: Zondervan, 1998.

Fields, Doug. *Your First Two Years in Youth Ministry: A Personal and Practical Guide to Starting Right*. Grand Rapids, MI: Zondervan, 2002.

Flores, Victor with Esther Flores. *Raise to Release: A Missional Mandate for Parents.* Houston, TX: Lucid Books, 2015.

Fowler, James W. *Stages of Faith: the Psychology of Human Development and the Quest for Meaning.* San Francisco, CA: Harper & Row, 1981.

Frost, Michael and Alan Hirsch. *ReJesus: A Wild Messiah for a Missional Church.* Peabody, MA: Hendrickson Publishers, 2009.

Gallaty, Robby. *Growing Up: How to be a Disciple Who Makes Disciples.* Bloomington, IN: CrossBooks, 2013.

Gallaty, Robby. *MARCS of a Disciple: A Biblical Guide for Gauging Spiritual Growth.* Hendersonville, TN: Replicate Ministries, 2016.

Gartman, Chuck and Richard Barnes. *Youth Sunday School for a New Century.* Nashville, TN: Broadman and Holman, 2001.

Geiger, Eric and Jeff Borton. *Simple Student Ministry.* Nashville, TN: B&H Publishing Group, 2009.

Greear, J.D. *Gospel: Recovering the Power that Made Christianity Revolutionary.* Nashville, TN: B&H Publishing Group, 2011.

Grudem, Wayne A. *Making Sense of the Church: One of Seven Parts from Grudem's Systematic Theology.* Grand Rapids, MI: Zondervan, 2011.

Grudem, Wayne. *Systematic Theology: An Introduction to Biblical Doctrine.* Grand Rapids, MI: Zondervan, 1995.

Ham, Ken and Britt Beemer. *Already Gone: Ways Your Kids Will Quit Church and What You Can Do about It.* Green Forest, AR: Master Books, 2009.

Hamilton, James in, Randy Stinson and Timothy Paul Jones, eds. *Trained in the Fear of God: Family Ministry in Theological, Historical, and Practical Perspective.* Grand Rapids, MI: Kregel Publishers, 2011.

Hammett, John S. "Human Nature," in *A Theology for the Church*, ed. Daniel Akin. Nashville, TN: Broadman and Holman Academic, 2007.

Harris, Alex and Brett. *Do Hard Things.* Colorado Springs, CO: Multnomah Books, 2008.

Higgs, Mike. *Youth Ministry on Your Knees: Mentoring and Motivating Youth to Pray.* Colorado Springs, CO: NavPress, 2004.

Hull, Bill. *The Complete Book of Discipleship: On Being and Making Followers of Christ.* Colorado Springs, CO: Navpress, 2006.

Hunter, Ron. "The D6 View of Youth Ministry," *Youth Ministry in the 21st Century: Five Views*, Chap Clark, ed. Grand Rapids, MI: Baker Academic, 2015.

Hutchcraft, Ron. *The Battleground for a Generation.* Chicago, IL: Moody Press, 1996.

Idleman, Kyle. *Not a Fan: Becoming a Completely Committed Follower of Jesus.* Grand Rapids, MI: Zondervan, 2011.

Jackson, Allen. "The Contribution of Teaching to Discipleship" in *Teaching the Next Generations: A Comprehensive Guide for Teaching Christian Formation.* Terry Linhart, ed. Grand Rapids, MI: Baker Academic, 2016.

Johnston, Kurt and Tim Levert. *The Nine Best Practices for Youth Ministry.* Loveland, CO: Group Publishing, 2010.

Jones, Timothy Paul, ed. *Perspectives on Family Ministry: 3 Views.* Nashville, TN: Holman Bible Publishers, 2009.

Kimmel, Tim. *Connecting Church and Home.* Nashville, TN: Randall House, 2013.

Kinnaman, David. *You Lost Me.* Grand Rapids, MI: Baker Publishing, 2011.

Küng, Huns. *Freud and the Problem of God*, translated by Edward Quinn. New Haven: Yale University Press, 1990.

Lawrence, Rick. *Jesus-Centered Youth Ministry.* Loveland, CO: Group Publishing, 2007.

Linhart, Terry, ed. *Teaching the Next Generations: A Comprehensive Guide for Teaching Christian Formation.* Grand Rapids, MI: Baker Academic, 2016.

Luther, Martin. *Commentary on Genesis, Vol. II - Luther on Sin and the Flood.* Minneapolis, MN: The Luther Press, 2010.

McDowell, Josh and Sean McDowell. *Experience Your Bible.* Eugene, OR: Harvest House Publishers, 2012.

McDowell, Josh. "Foreword," in David Noebel and Chuck Edwards. *Thinking like a Christian: Understanding and Living a Biblical Worldview.* Nashville, TN: B&H Publishing Group, 2002.

Martinson, Roland, Wesley Black, and John Roberto. *The Spirit and Culture of Youth Ministry: Leading Congregations toward Exemplary Youth Ministry.* St. Paul, MN: EYM Publishing, 2010.

Matlock, Mark. *Generation Hope.* Friendswood, TX: Baxter Press, 2002.

Mayo, Jeanne. *Thriving Youth Groups*. Loveland, CO: Group Publishing, 2005.

Mims, Gene. *Kingdom Principles for Church Growth*. Nashville, TN: LifeWay Christian Resources, 1994.

Mueller, Walt. *Engaging the Soul of Youth Culture*. Downers Grove, IL: InterVarsity Press, 2006.

Nishioka, Rodger. "Theological Foundation for Youth Ministry: Grace" in *Starting Right: Thinking Theologically about Youth Ministry*, ed. Kenda Dean, Chap Clark, and Dave Rahn. Grand Rapids, MI: Zondervan, 2001.

Ogden, Greg. *Transforming Discipleship*. Downers Grove, IL: InterVarsity Press, 2003.

O'Neil, Mary K. and Salman Akhtar, *On Freud's The Future of An Illusion*. London: Karnac Books, 2009.

Parr, Steve R. and Tom Crites. *Why They Stay: Helping Parents and Church Leaders Make Investments That Keep Children and Teens Connected to the Church for a Lifetime*. Bloomington, IN: WestBow Press, 2015.

Pearcey, Nancy. *Total Truth: Liberating Christianity from Its Cultural Captivity*. Wheaton, IL: Crossway Books, 2004.

Platt, David. *Radical*. Colorado Springs, CO: Multnomah Press, 2010.

Powell, Kara, Jake Mulder, and Brad Griffin. *Growing Young: Six Essential Strategies*. Grand Rapids, MI: Baker Books, 2016.

Powell, Kara, Brad Griffin, and Cheryl Crawford. *Sticky Faith*. Grand Rapids, MI: Zondervan, 2011.

Rahn, Dave and Terry Linhart. *Evangelism Remixed: Empowering Students for Courageous and Contagious Faith*. Grand Rapids, MI: Zondervan, 2009.

Reeves, Michael. *Rejoicing in Christ*. Downers Grove, IL: InterVarsity Press, 2015.

Reid, Alvin. *Evangelism Handbook*. B&H Publishing Group, 2009.

Reid, Alvin L. *Raising the Bar: Ministry to Youth in the New Millennium*. Grand Rapids, MI: Kregel, 2004.

Rienow, Rob. *Five Reasons for Spiritual Apathy in Teens*. Nashville, TN: Randall House, 2015.

Rienow, Rob. *Limited Church: Unlimited Kingdom*. Nashville, TN: Randall House, 2013.

Rienow, Rob. *Visionary Parenting*. Nashville, TN: Randall House, 2009.

Robbins, Duffy. *Building a Youth Ministry That Builds Disciples*. Grand Rapids, MI: Zondervan, 2011.

Ross, Richard ed. *Accelerate: Parenting Teenagers Toward Adulthood*. Nashville, TN: LifeWay, 2015.

Ross, Richard. *The Senior Pastor and the Reformation of Youth Ministry*. Nashville, TN: LifeWay, 2015.

Ross, Richard. *Student Ministry and the Supremacy of Christ*. Nashville, TN: LifeWay, 2015.

Schultz, Glen. *Kingdom Education*. Nashville, TN: LifeWay Press, 2002.

Senter, Mark H., ed. *Four Views of Youth Ministry and the Church*. Grand Rapids, MI: Zondervan, 2001.

Shafer, Barry. *Unleashing God's Word in Youth Ministry*. Grand Rapids, MI: Zondervan, 2008.

Smith, Christian with Melinda Lundquist Denton. *Soul Searching: The Religious and Spiritual Lives of American Teenagers*. New York: Oxford University Press, 2005.

Smith, Tim. *8 Habits of an Effective Youth Worker*. Wheaton, IL: Victor Books, 1995.

Sneed, Barry and Roy Edgemon. *Transformational Discipleship*. Nashville, TN: LifeWay, 1999.

Spurgeon, C.H. *Lectures to My Students*. Grand Rapids, MI: Zondervan, 1972.

Steinberg, Laurence. *Adolescence*, 8th ed. New York: McGraw Hill, 2008.

Stier, Greg. "A Gospel-Advancing Ministry Model," *Youth Ministry in the 21st Century: Five Views*, ed. Chap Clark. Grand Rapids, MI: Baker Academic, 2015.

Stier, Greg. *Gospelize Your Youth Ministry*. Arvada, CO: Dare 2 Share, 2015.

Stier, Greg. *Outbreak: Creating a Contagious Youth Ministry through Viral Evangelism*. Chicago, IL: Moody Press, 2002.

Strommen, Merton P. and Richard A. Hardel, *Passing On the Faith: A Radical New Model for Youth and Family Ministry*. Minnesota: Saint Mary's Press, 2000).

Sulloway, Frank J. *Freud, Biologist of the Mind: Beyond the Psychoanalytic Legend*. Cambridge, MA: Harvard University Press, 1992.

Swindoll, Charles R. *Grace Awakening*. Nashville, TN: Thomas Nelson, 2003.

Thiselton, Anthony C. *Systematic Theology*. Grand Rapids, MI: Eerdmans, 2015.

Trueblood, Ben. *Student Ministry That Matters: Three Elements of a Healthy Student Ministry*. Nashville, TN: LifeWay, 2016.

West, John G. *Darwin Day in America: How Our Politics and Culture Have Been Dehumanized in the Name of Science*. Wilmington, DE: ISI Books, 2007.

Wilcher, Scott. *The Orphaned Generation: The Father's Heart for Connecting Youth and Young Adults to Your Church*. Chesapeake, VA: UpStream Project, 2010.

Wilkins, Michael J. *Following the Master: A Biblical Theology of Discipleship*. Grand Rapids, MI; Zondervan, 1992.

Willard, Dallas. *The Divine Conspiracy: Rediscovering Our Hidden Life in God*. New York: HarperCollins Publishers, 1998.

Willard, Dallas. *Renovation of the Heart: Putting on the Character of Christ*. Colorado Springs, CO: Navpress, 2002.

Wright, N.T. *Simply Jesus: A New Vision of Who He Was, What He Did, and Why He Matters*. New York: HarperCollins, 2011.

Zirschky, Andrew. *Beyond the Screen: Youth Ministry for the Connected but Alone Generation.* Nashville, TN: Abington Press, 2015.

Zock, Hetty. *A Psychology of Ultimate Concern: Erik H. Erikson's Contribution to the Psychology of Religion.* New York: Rodopi, 2004.

Journals and Periodicals

Beaty, Katelyn, "Lost in Transition." *Christianity Today*, 53 (10).

Gentry, Peter J. "Raising Children, the Christian Way" *The Journal of Discipleship and Family Ministry* 2.2. (2012).

Goodwin, Antoinette. "Freud and Erikson: their Contributions to the Psychology of God-Image Formation," *Pastoral Psychology*, 47 (1998): 101.

Snailum, Brenda. "Implementing Intergenerational Youth Ministry within Existing Evangelical Church Congregations: What Have We Learned?," *Christian Education Journal* 9, no. 1 (2012).

Websites

Allen, David. "Text-Driven Preaching and Pragmatic Textual Analysis." January 7, 2014. theologicalmatters.com.

Allen, David. "Text-Driven Preaching and Sermon Form." October 1, 2013. theologicalmatters.com

Barna Group. "Five Myths about Young Adult Church Dropouts." November 16, 2011. barna.org.

Barna Group. "5 Ways to Connect with Millennials." September 9, 2014. barna.org.

Barna, George. "The Priorities, Challenges, and Trends in Youth Ministry." April 6, 2016. barna.org.

Barna, George. "Research Shows Parenting Approach Determines Whether Children Become Devoted Christians." April 9, 2007. barna.org.

Barna, George. "Spiritual Progress Hard to Find in 2003." December 22, 2003. barna.org.

Bryant, David. "Why Our Mission Is so Critical." July 20, 2014. proclaimhope.org.

Edwards, Jonathan. "Farewell Sermon," accessed September 19, 2016. sermonaudio.com.

Elliff, Tom. "First-Person: Has Your Family Heard Your Testimony?" January 10, 2003. bpnews.net.

Epstein, Robert. "The Myth of the Teen Brain." June 1, 2007. scientificamerican.com.

Kinnaman, David. "Most Twentysomethings Put Christianity on the Shelf Following Spiritually Active Teen Years." September 11, 2006. barna.org.

Mueller, Walt. "Why Youth Ministry Shouldn't Be the Greatest Show on Earth." June 1, 2017. cpyu.org.

The Nielsen Company. "Cross-Platform Report," accessed February 9, 2017. nielsen.com.

Revell, John. "As You Are Going, Make Disciples—Starting in the Home!" June 2001. sbclife.net.